The Texas State Capitol

The Texas State Capitol

Selected Essays from the
Southwestern Historical Quarterly

Texas State Historical Association
Austin

The essays in this book were originally published in the October 1988
and April 1992 issues of the *Southwestern Historical Quarterly*.

ISBN 0-87611-150-9

10 9 8 7 6 5 4 3 2 1

Published by the Texas State Historical Association in cooperation with
the Center for Studies in Texas History at the University of Texas at
Austin.

This book is number fourteen in the Fred H. and Ella Mae Moore Texas
History Reprint Series.

The paper used in this book meets the minimum requirements of the
American National Standard for Permanence of Paper for Printed
Library Materials, Z39.48—1984.

Cover: The Texas State Capitol. *Photograph by J. Griffis Smith. Courtesy Texas
Department of Transportation.*

Contents

Pride of Texas: The State Capitol

WILLARD B. ROBINSON*

THROUGHOUT THE WESTERN WORLD, PUBLIC BUILDINGS HAVE LONG been viewed as reflections of the attainments of civilized societies. An unknown Galveston newspaper reporter set the stage for the new Texas State Capitol when he wrote in 1880, "The public buildings of a state are its most pronounced features, and by them the character and genius of the people are largely judged by outsiders."[1] Like so many others, he sensed that architecture served as a barometer—the size, opulence, and style of a building represented a scale of social values. The most important functions of society were housed in the largest and finest buildings.

Americans have historically erected imposing statehouses that reflect their esteem for democratic government. Representatives of Texas government consistently dedicated their energies to the construction of one of the finest statehouses in the world in the late nineteenth century. Through its majestic form and monumental style, its furnishings, landscaping, and artwork, the Texas State Capitol (erected 1882–1888) reflected the pride of Texas citizens in the culture and government of their state.

While buildings were considered reflections of cultural and political values during the nineteenth century, they were also viewed as influences upon human attitudes. This disposition was represented by one early nineteenth-century writer who opined that when objects of beauty are placed "before the public . . . the sure consequence will be, a refinement of taste, an elevation of mental character. . . ."[2] Another writer observed that architecture "has been regarded as so direct a means of inspiring the imagination, and creating sublime ideas in the mind, as to be assigned . . . to a high place among those causes which affect the

*Willard B. Robinson is the Paul Whitfield Horn Professor of Architecture at Texas Tech University.

[1] From the Houston *Daily Post*, printed in the *Daily Democrat* (Fort Worth), Dec. 4, 1880.

[2] "Architecture in the United States," *American Journal of Science and Arts*, XVII (1829), 109.

character of an age, and exert a prominent influence over the moral and intellectual habits of a people."[3] Perhaps such perceptions at least touched the minds of Texas officials at mid-century, when they turned their thoughts to the construction of the first permanent Capitol in Austin. This building replaced a temporary one-story wooden structure erected in 1839.[4]

The opportunity to construct an impressive Capitol came with the cession of lands that extended west and north of the present state boundary lines. As compensation for these lands, the federal government awarded the state of Texas $10,000,000, plus interest. Early in 1852 the legislature appropriated $100,000 from this sum for a new capitol, along with $25,000 for its furnishings.[5]

Commissioners appointed to oversee the construction invited plans from interested builders.[6] For whatever reasons, however, they evidently were not satisfied with the submissions. According to the *Texas Republican* (Marshall), they "rejected all the plans submitted, *borowing* (*?*) [*sic*] enough from each to enable them to draft one of their *own*."[7] The commissioners contracted the stonework to O. J. Nichols and the woodwork to Abner H. Cook; the building under their purview was occupied in 1853, although still incomplete.[8]

Located on "Capitol Square," a four-block eminence reserved for the principal state governmental structure in the original plan (1840) of Austin (fig. 1), the edifice was an impressive work in Greek Revival

---

[3] "Architecture in the United States," *North American Review*, LVIII (Apr., 1844), 436.

[4] For an early description of the wooden Capitol see Francis Moore, Jr., *Map and Description . . .* (Philadelphia: H. Tanner, Junr., 1840), 130.
The various capitols of Texas have been surveyed in several publications, including: Robert C. Cotner, *The Texas State Capitol* (Austin: Pemberton Press, 1968); Sara Clark, *The Capitols of Texas: A Visual History* (Austin: Encino Press, 1975); Seymour V. Connor et al., *Capitols of Texas* (Waco: Texian Press, 1970); Texas Legislative Council, *The Texas Capitol: Symbol of Accomplishment* (4th ed.; Austin: Texas Legislative Council, 1986). See also Henry-Russell Hitchcock and William Seale, *Temples of Democracy: The State Capitols of the USA* (New York: Harcourt Brace Jovanovich, 1976), 182–188, and Willard B. Robinson, *Texas Public Buildings of the Nineteenth Century* (Austin: University of Texas Press for Amon Carter Museum of Western Art, 1974), 27, 206, 260–265.

[5] August Watkins Harris, *Minor and Major Mansions and Their Companions in Early Austin: A Sequel* (Austin: August Watkins Harris, 1958), n.p. Harris provides conjectural plans for this building.

[6] For several centuries architectural competitions had been a common means of selecting architects of important public buildings. The architect of the dome of the Florence Cathedral, Felippo Brunelleschi, for instance, was selected through competition. Similarly, the design by William Thornton for the United States Capitol was selected by a committee from a group of plans submitted by several architects. Eventually throughout the United States countless church and civic-building architects were selected by this means.

[7] *Texas Republican* (Marshall), Apr. 17, 1852. No reasons for their action were given, although the reporter noted that one was rejected because "it was too good. . . ." Ostensibly, the estimated cost of the buildings would have been greater than the appropriation. John Brandon, a builder, is sometimes given credit for the final design of the structure.

[8] Ibid., June 16, 1855.

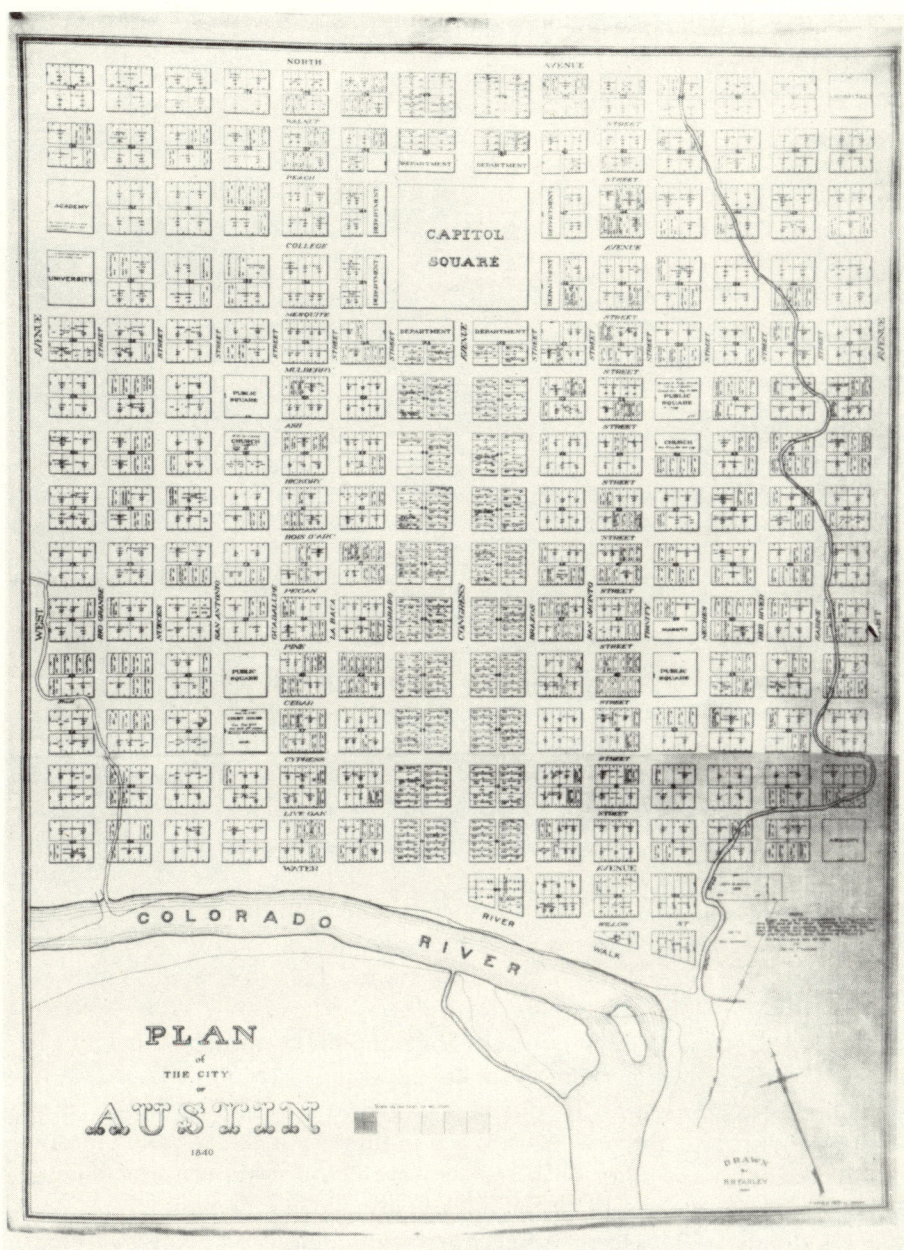

Figure 1. *Plan of the City of Austin* by H. H. Farley, 1840. Ink on paper, 26½ ×
17¾ inches. *Courtesy General Land Office, Austin.*

Figure 2. Photograph (c. 1876) of the Texas Capitol that was begun in 1852.
Courtesy Archives Division, Texas State Library, Austin.

style, with exterior walls of soft yellow limestone (fig. 2). Walls had horizontal rustication on the bottom story and smooth stonework on the upper stories. Frederick Law Olmsted described it as "a really imposing building. . . ."[9] With similar sympathies, a romantic newspaper reporter saw it as an edifice "which strikes with instant and pleasing effect the eye of the beholder."[10] In reality, however, the building lacked the aesthetic sophistication of a number of other state capitols dating from the first half of the century.

On an oblong plan about 90 feet wide and 145 feet long, the interior spaces were oriented to a central hall, announced on the outside by a monumental portico approached by a wide flight of steps. The first floor housed state offices; the second, both the Senate chamber and "Hall of Representatives"; and the third, a library and museum.[11]

Although at first acclaimed for its imposing form, the edifice eventually lost its appeal as dreams of a larger structure crystalized. After the building was destroyed by a fire ignited by a faulty stovepipe installation on November 9, 1881, one reporter denounced it as having had "a startling resemblance to a large sized corn crib, with a pumpkin for a dome. . . ."[12] He merely echoed the opinions of others who had

[9] Frederick Law Olmsted, *A Journey through Texas; or, A Saddle-Trip on the Southwestern Frontier . . .* (New York: Dix, Edwards & Co., 1857), 110.

[10] *Texas Republican* (Marshall), June 16, 1855.

[11] Ibid.; *The Texas Almanac for 1858 . . .* (Galveston: Richardson & Co., 1857), 90 (quotation).

[12] "When the Old Capitol Burned," 8 (unidentified newspaper clipping in author's files).

Figure 3. View of the temporary Capitol of Texas constructed in 1883. From *Art Work of Austin* (Chicago: W. H. Parish Publishing Co., 1894). *Courtesy Austin History Center, Austin Public Library.*

begun agitating for a new building, claiming the old structure was functionally and aesthetically obsolete.

Soon after the Greek Revival temple was lost, Frederick E. Ruffini, an Austin architect, was commissioned to design a temporary Capitol (fig. 3).[13] Located across Congress Avenue from the Travis County Courthouse at the foot of Capitol Hill, the structure was dedicated on January 1, 1883.[14] Although a temporary statehouse, it was handsomely designed in Italianate style with a cut-stone façade, three stories high. While work progressed on the permanent Capitol, the executive department occupied the first floor; the legislative, the second; and the judicial, the third.[15]

---

[13] Immediately after the Greek Revival edifice was destroyed, the Senate met in the Armory and the House in Millett's Opera House. *Burke's Texas Almanac and Immigrant's Handbook for 1883* . . . (Houston: J. Burke, 1882), 37.

[14] Fort Worth *Daily Gazette*, Jan. 2, 1883.

[15] After the permanent Capitol was completed, the temporary Capitol was occupied by the Austin Public School System. The building was destroyed by fire in 1899. Construction was described in *Report of Construction of the Temporary State Capitol at Austin, Texas* (Austin: E. W. Swindells, State Printer, 1883). For a history of the temporary Capitol, see Gary L. Moore et al., *Temporary Capitol of Texas, 1883–88: History and Archaeology*, Texas Highway Department Pub-

Cries for a new permanent Capitol that would project a fitting image of the Lone Star State had been heard prior to the loss of the Greek Revival edifice. Well aware of the needs of the state, both practical and symbolic, the Texas legislature had already passed "An Act to provide for building a new State Capitol" in 1879. The legislation created a Capitol Board, consisting of the governor, treasurer, comptroller, attorney-general, and commissioner of the Land Office to oversee execution of the work. The board then appointed a building superintendent and two commissioners, who were to solicit plans and select an architect.[16]

In 1875, to pay for the building, the state had set aside 3 million acres of land, at the time a plentiful reserve, rather than money. In 1879 an additional 50,000 acres were designated to pay for a survey of the land. The land thus reserved for the Capitol project was located in the Panhandle adjacent to New Mexico in the west and to Indian Territory in the north.[17]

With means for financing at hand, the building commission undertook the task of selecting an architect, evidently after consultation with several local firms that assisted in the development of a design program. The process was formally initiated late in 1880 with a publication describing the project and with newspaper advertisements of a national competition. Intent upon attracting talented architects, the commissioners offered a prize of $1,700 to the winning design, a paltry sum for the effort required.[18] Evidently recognizing their own limitations in judging architectural quality, and at the request of Texas governor Oran M. Roberts, they appointed Napoléon Le Brun, a prestigious New York architect, as consultant to assist in the selection of a winner and to make recommendations on design refinements. From eleven entries, each submitted anonymously, Le Brun chose the proposal of Elijah E. Myers, a Detroit architect who had designed, among other important buildings, the Michigan State Capitol (1872–1879). The two

lications in Archaeology, No. 1 (Austin: Texas Highway Department, 1972). The specifications were published as *Contracts for Building the Temporary State Capitol at Austin, Texas* (Austin: State Printing Office, D. & D. Institution, 1882).

[16] *Report of the Capitol Building Commissioners to the Governor of Texas, Austin, January 1, 1883* (Austin: E. W. Swindells, State Printer, 1883), 9–10.

[17] Ibid., 3–6; Frederick W. Rathjen, "The Texas State House: A Study of the Building of the Texas Capitol Based on the Reports of the Capitol Building Commissioners," *Southwestern Historical Quarterly*, LX (Apr., 1957), 435. Situated in ten counties, the land was eventually developed into the famous XIT Ranch, with assistance from English capital. For a history, see J. Evetts Haley, *The XIT Ranch of Texas, and the Early Days of the Llano Estacado* (Chicago: Lakeside Press, 1929).

[18] For a discussion of the competition, see "The Texas Capitol Competition," *American Architect and Building News*, XII (Sept. 30, 1882), 154.

commissioners endorsed Le Brun's decision, and the board agreed to pay a commission of $12,000.[19]

Soon Myers's office was busily engaged in preparing the contract documents. Myers incorporated several changes recommended by Le Brun and others suggested by the board, including adjustments in proportions and alterations of the dome. The working drawings were drafted in ink on large linen sheets, which are now deposited in the State Archives (fig. 4). These plans, along with the specifications, were made available to bidders on July 1, 1881. Since contractors were to be compensated in acreage rather than money, the winning bid would be the one that specified the smallest number of acres rather than the lowest cost. On January 1, 1882, Mattheas Schnell of Rock Island, Illinois, one of only two bidders, was awarded the contract. Subsequently he assigned his interest to Taylor, Babcock, and Company, which in turn assigned its interest to Abner Taylor. Excavations for the foundation commenced in 1882, north of the burnt ruins of the old Capitol, but the cornerstone was not placed until March 2, 1885.[20]

As was common with large projects, construction was beset with numerous problems, many of which were kept constantly before the public by the press. Among the most controversial, both aesthetically and symbolically, was a decision stipulating the type of stone to be employed for the exterior veneer. Specifications called for local light gray limestone, but it was soon found that the supply of stone uniform in color was insufficient and that the local material contained iron, which oxidized when exposed to the elements, resulting in discoloration.[21] A recommendation by the building commission in June, 1885, to use Bedford limestone from Indiana incited public outrage against nondomestic material. Finally a proposal to use Texas red granite, a durable and attractive stone, proved acceptable. Because of the difficulty and cost of carving the material, however, concessions were made in design and construction. Rock-faced ashlar with margins was substituted for smooth sand-rubbed ashlar. Porticoes on the east and west were eliminated, and the Corinthian order, commonly used for important public buildings, was replaced by a simplified version of the Doric

[19] Allen Stross, *The Michigan State Capitol* (Lansing: Michigan Historical Commission, 1969), 38; *Report of the Capitol Building Commissioners* (1883), 21.

[20] *Report of the Capitol Building Commissioners* (1883), 22, 29, 31, 52; Austin *Daily Statesman*, Mar. 3, 1885.

[21] The exterior required 3,000 carloads of stone. Another 12,000 carloads were required for other parts of the building.

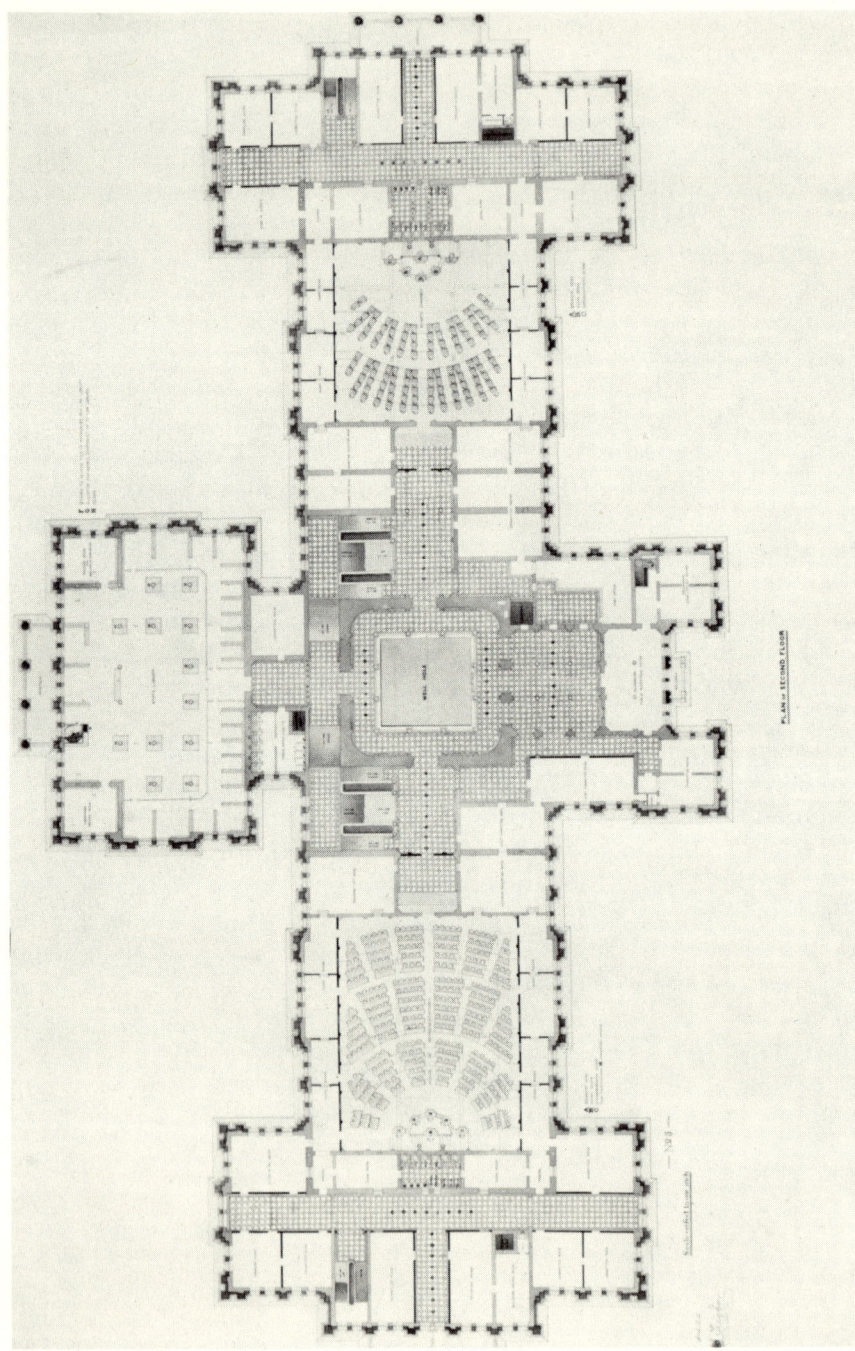

Figure 4. Architect Elijah E. Myers's working drawing of the Capitol. Colored ink on paper, 24⅛ × 38⅜ inches. *Courtesy Archives Division, Texas State Library, Austin.*

Figure 5. This view of the Capitol, a detail from Augustus Koch's 1887 bird's-eye view of Austin, was evidently based on Myers's working drawings since it shows neither changes in the dome nor the elimination of the east and west porticos. *Courtesy Historic American Buildings Survey (HABS), Library of Congress.*

order—all of which, interestingly, produced a unique Capitol, distinguished not only by its size but also by color and detail (fig. 5).[22]

There were also structural problems, which involved the support of the tremendously heavy dome (fig. 4). In 1887 architects B. M. Harrod of New Orleans, Nicholas J. Clayton of Galveston, and Eugene T. Heiner of Houston were invited to inspect the structure, which appeared weak, and to make recommendations about strengthening it. Following their advice, some ironwork was strengthened and several alterations in construction were made.[23]

----

[22] The controversy over the type of stone was detailed in many newspapers. See, for example, the Fort Worth *Daily Gazette*, June 23, 28, July 11, 22, 1885; Galveston *Daily News*, July 13, 18, 25, 1885. Among other concessions, the state agreed to furnish a quarry and convict labor, which resulted in further disputes. See Robinson, *Texas Public Buildings of the Nineteenth Century*, 261, and Texas Legislative Council, *The Texas Capitol*, 50–51. Incidentally, similar porticoes can be viewed on the Colorado State Capitol (1886–1908), also designed by Elijah Myers.

[23] For their report, see *Report of the Capitol Building Commission, upon the Completion of the New Capitol, Comprising the Reports of the Commissioners, Superintendent and Secretary, to the Governor of Texas, on the Occasion of the Covening of the Twentieth Legislature in Extra Session, April 16, 1888* (Austin: Hutchings Printing House, 1888), 68–73.

In spite of these and numerous other difficulties—including disputes with architect Myers, who was finally dismissed—the monumental Capitol was completed in 1888. On May 16 it was presented by the contractor to the people of Texas and dedicated by the Masonic Grand Lodge with all the pomp and pageantry fitting a supreme public accomplishment. Civic and military demonstrations, parades, fireworks, and musical performances celebrated the new statehouse. Thousands of yards of bunting waved in the streets of Austin.[24]

The building was soon extolled for its size and beauty. Its overall length was set at 562 feet and its depth at 287 feet; the distance from a base line to the gilded star of galvanized sheet metal held aloft by the Goddess of Liberty on the dome was recorded as 311 feet above ground level, surpassing by several feet the height of the National Capitol. The magnitude of the accomplishment was acknowledged by the commission, which reported, "Of all similar structures in America, it is second in size only to the National Capitol. . . ." *Frank Leslie's Illustrated Newspaper* ranked the building "among the really great structures of the world." Some newspapers boasted it was the "noblest edifice upon this hemisphere. . . ." Finally, in an official report, Mifflin E. Bell, a former supervising architect for the United States Treasury, described it as "both awe inspiring and grand in its effect upon the mind of the most technical critic."[25]

The imposing edifice so admired both then and now is a grandiose work in Renaissance Revival style, incorporating academic design principles of the École des Beaux Arts (fig. 6). It consists of a large projecting central block with wings extending east and west, a compositional scheme similar to the National Capitol and also found in the Michigan State Capitol. The paired columns and large arch on the south side recall the triumphal arches of Roman antiquity, which became common features on both Italian and French Renaissance churches. Supported by a colonnaded drum and capped by a lantern, a large, well-proportioned dome at once unifies the massive composition and proclaims its governmental purpose. On the south side the impressive triumphal arch, a processional form, along with a small portico, boldly announces the entrance (fig. 6). Opposite on the north is a grand portico, composed of a

---

24 The Fort Worth *Daily Gazette*, May 18, 1888, describes the event in detail.

25 *Report of the Capitol Building Commissioners* (1883), 48 (1st quotation); *Frank Leslie's Illustrated Newspaper*, May 12, 1888, p. 203 (2nd quotation); Fort Worth *Daily Gazette*, May 18, 1888 (3rd quotation); "Report of M. E. Bell, Architect, on the Construction of the Capitol Building," Dec. 3, 1888, in *Final Report of the Secretary of [the] State Capitol Board, Austin, December 18, 1888* (Austin: State Printing Office, 1888), 16.

Figure 6. This view of the Capitol, taken from the southeast, was photographed by Todd Webb c. 1965–1966. *Courtesy Amon Carter Museum, Fort Worth, Texas.*

loggia arcade on the ground floor and a colonnaded loggia above. The wings extending from the central mass terminate at pavilions, affording convenient access to public functions on the ground level, including museums for both the geologist and adjutant general, and creating a five-part form. Accented by flanking paired columns, slight projections of the wings between the central mass and end pavilions mark important offices on the ground level, such as those of the secretary of state.

The design of the exterior walls conforms to the Classical formula for vertical composition (beginning, middle, and end). The ground story serves as a base, emphasized by rustication, which gives an appearance of strength. Above, pilasters extend two stories, forming the middle and contributing to the monumental image. These pilasters are surmounted by a large, well-proportioned entablature, capping the walls of the three-story wings. A second entablature terminates the central mass.

Although the design of the Capitol is based upon traditional composition, modern technology played an important role in the building's construction. The structure of the dome, for instance, is wrought iron, as is much of the framing elsewhere (fig. 7). Originally wrought iron was also specified for the outer shell of the dome, but galvanized sheet iron was finally substituted for wrought iron in the entablature sup-

Figure 7. View of the Capitol rotunda by Todd Webb, c. 1965–1966. *Courtesy Amon Carter Museum, Fort Worth, Texas.*

ported by the colonnade and for the outer surface of the dome, resulting in a reduction of weight and a saving of time in construction, both of which were considered very important. Thus, the outer surface of the dome and its supporting drum are actually metal, painted to give the appearance of stone construction. On the interior, cast-iron components manufactured in the foundry of the East Texas Penitentiary at Rusk were employed for columns. Galvanized iron, pressed into intricate patterns, was also installed for the ceilings of the Senate and House.

The interior spatial plan was formally developed along major and minor axes, with a hierarchical organization emphasizing various functions. Aligned with Congress Avenue, the major (short) axis on the ground level extends from the triumphal arch through a colonnaded lobby to the rotunda, the ceremonial focal space and nucleus of the

Figure 8. View of the first floor corridor by Todd Webb, c. 1965–1966. *Courtesy Amon Carter Museum, Fort Worth, Texas.*

building and an area intended to impress visitors.[26] Intersecting the major axis at the rotunda is the minor (long) axis, a corridor along which offices are located (fig. 8). Adjacent to the rotunda, grand stairways constructed with cast iron communicate with the second floor, where the state library was situated and where the governor's public reception room is located on the major axis, with a view of Congress Avenue to the south. On this floor, vestibules adjacent to the rotunda open into the House of Representatives on the west and the Senate on the east. Centered upon the long axis, their hierarchical position is emphasized by their location on the second floor, which can be identified from the exterior as the *piano nobile*. The chambers culminate a public spatial sequence, a *grand marche* through the triumphal arch, lobby, rotunda, stairway, and vestibule to the legislative hall. The grand stairs, along with other secondary stairs, continue to the third story, where the judicial department, with its Supreme and appellate courtrooms and law library, was situated.

The walk through the Capitol is highlighted by a variety of ornamental features, also intended to inspire and impress. In both the south

[26] The interior of the dome had evidently been intended for allegorical and historical painted scenes, similar in idea to numerous domes in Europe.

Figure 9. View of the Senate chamber by Jack E. Boucher, 1966. *Courtesy HABS.*

lobby and the rotunda, sculptures and paintings of prominent Texans evoke patriotic thoughts that bolster feelings of pride and unity. Moving along the first-floor corridor, the visitor finds doors decorated with fine Classical details executed in oak and pine, which signify the dignity of the offices beyond (fig. 8). Fine details also enhance the entrances to the Senate chamber and the House of Representatives.[27]

Both the Senate, ninety-four feet by seventy feet, and the House, ninety-four feet square, are magnificent two-story spaces with galleries. The chambers are decorated with Renaissance themes that are consistent with the exterior (figs. 9, 10). Decorative Corinthian pilasters supporting full entablatures articulate the enclosing walls. Overhead, a coffered ceiling with pendants contributes to the richness of the setting. Originally, both rooms were lighted naturally by skylights of embossed (acid-etched) glass and by windows, which also allowed good cross ventilation in the days before air conditioning. Roof ventilators provided additional air circulation. Gas lighting was used in the vaults and entrance, and temporary arc lights were used elsewhere, but these were

---

[27] In 1888, an initial appropriation of $10,000 was made to purchase "pictures and statuary of men prominent in history. . . ." *Report of a Board to Purchase Pictures, Etc., Created by Act of May 17, 1888* (Austin: State Printing Office, 1889), 3. Similar doors are found in the Michigan State Capitol.

Figure 10. View of the House of Representatives chamber by Jack E. Boucher, 1966. *Courtesy HABS.*

soon replaced by electric lighting. Electric lights were installed in the legislative halls in 1899, the electricity being supplied by a generator.[28]

At the dedication of the building, these impressive spaces were without furniture. Soon desks, tables, chairs, and other items complementing the functional heirarchy of the various offices and departments were manufactured and delivered.

The Capitol is a unique statement composed of a universal Classical vocabulary. The familiar forms and details provide intelligible meaning and beauty (unlike much of today's architecture, which fails to communicate). History provides the details and intellectual associations essential to this understanding. A Renaissance Revival dome, for example, conveys both the purpose and importance of the edifice.

The long axial form of the Texas statehouse is obviously based upon the National Capitol and is also similar to a number of other state capitols. The crowning dome over a rotunda, with the Senate chamber and House of Representatives located in opposite wings, became a standard

---

[28] The building was both plumbed for gas-light fixtures and wired for electrical lights. Plumbing provided for some 3,200 gas fixtures. *Report of the Capitol Building Commission* (1888), 22, 25. The building was also wired for 1,300 incandescent lamps, although the generator could power only 650 lamps at any one time. *Report of the Board for Fencing and Improving the Capitol Grounds, November, 1890* (Austin: State Printing Office, 1890), 4.

scheme, reflecting democratic government. The dome, with its Corinthian colonnaded drum and its hemispherical ribbed form, closely resembles that of the National Capitol (1855–1863), which was influenced by St. Paul's Cathedral, London (1675), and the Pantheon, Paris (1757–1790). The Armed Liberty that surmounts the National Capitol and accents the skyline of Washington, D.C., has a counterpart in the Goddess of Liberty that at one time was the dominant accent of the Austin skyline. The proportions of the two statues differ, however, having been carefully adjusted to the scales of their respective buildings.

Like the National Capitol, the Texas statehouse occupies a topographic eminence that complements its monumentality. Soon after the Texas edifice was dedicated, legislators turned their thoughts to landscaping the grounds. With an appropriation of $35,000, a board created to fence and improve the Capitol grounds contracted for early improvements. In 1889–1890 a wall was built with a granite coping and an iron fence.[29] Eventually trees and shrubs were installed, providing shade, color, and spatial organization to Capitol Square. Several monuments, including the memorial to the battle of the Alamo (1891), were also added.

Durably built, the Texas Capitol has proved to be functionally adaptable to most needs for a century, attesting to the foresight of those who created the design, those who executed it, and those who have maintained it. Nonetheless, changing times have required alterations, with some damage to the structural fabric of the building. Among the alterations are the extensive partitioning of original rooms to provide additional offices and the creation of wooden mezzanine levels, as well as installation of air conditioning, fluorescent light fixtures, and suspended acoustical ceilings.

Without question, the change most vividly affecting the appearance of the interior was the replacement of the original encaustic tile. In 1936 terrazzo designs by Harold E. ("Bubi") Jessen were installed on the first floor according to the plans and specifications of Charles H. Page, Sr. (fig. 8).[30] Designs rendered in intense hues in the south lobby commemorate famous battles, while those in the rotunda depict the seals of the six nations that had sovereignty over Texas.

Other work has been necessitated by accident. In 1983 a fire extensively damaged rooms in the east wing in back of the Senate chamber. This area was rehabilitated with designs by the late Lawrence D. White

---

[29] *Report of the Board for Fencing and Improving the Capitol Grounds,* 3.
[30] Texas Legislative Council, *The Texas Capitol,* 98.

of Lawrence D. White Associates, Inc., and Gerling-Thomas-Ward, Inc., consulting engineers.

Undoubtedly the fire alerted many people to the need for an organized program for architectural conservation and restoration, rather than piecemeal repairs and remodeling. In 1983, following the fire, the State Preservation Board was created by the legislature to "preserve, maintain, and restore the State Capitol"—certainly a noteworthy event in historic preservation in the state. To assist planning and implementation, this act also created a seven-member advisory committee.[31] The board was authorized to employ an architect of the Capitol to oversee the building and a curator of the Capitol to oversee its contents.

Following a precedent established in New York, the act creating the State Preservation Board calls for the development of a twenty-year master plan, phased for "the maintenance, preservation, restoration, and modification" of the building.[32] The Capitol architect, selected on the basis of qualifications recommended by the Texas Historical Commission, is charged with the responsibility of developing this plan, which will result in the complete restoration of the Capitol and the updating of safety features.

To provide documentation useful in the implementation of the master plan, the State Preservation Board initiated a project in 1986 to record the building with measured drawings through the Historic American Buildings Survey (HABS), a branch of the National Park Service. Although the original plans for the building exist, no formal record is available of changes made during construction in the 1880s. For instance, there are no drawings showing some of the original decorative work and the change from limestone to granite veneer, and there are few building cross-sections showing vertical characteristics. Prepared by students under the direction of an architecture professor, the drawings will be essential to the restoration planning (fig. 11). The originals, drafted in ink on mylar sheets in conformance with formal guidelines established by HABS, and field notes will be permanently deposited in the Library of Congress, where they will be available to scholars and other interested individuals. One of the largest and most

---

[31] SB 147, Sections 1 (quotation), 4. The board consists of the governor, who serves as chairman; lieutenant governor; Speaker of the house; and three appointed members. The governor, lieutenant governor, and Speaker of the house each appoint one member of the advisory committee. The other members of the committee are the directors of the Antiquities Committee, Texas Commission on the Arts, Texas Historical Commission, and Texas State Library and Archives Commission.

[32] Bob Mabry to Curtis Tunnell, Jan. 25, 1984 (Texas Antiquities Committee, Austin); SB 147, Section 6 (quotation).

DOME SECTION   SCALE   FEET 1/8"= 1'- 0"

METERS 1:96

TEXAS STATE CAPITOL

Figure 11. This computer-plotted drawing of the Capitol's dome was made in 1987 by the Historic American Buildings Survey. *Courtesy HABS.*

complex projects undertaken by a HABS team, this endeavor was begun in 1986 and continued the following year. Of particular note in this project was the use of a Computer-Aided Drafting and Design (CADD) program. The project was scheduled to continue during 1988. The computerized drawings will be used as base sheets for the documentation of various building systems, for artwork and furniture inventory, for all future restoration and remodeling, and for documentation of the historical evolution of the building and grounds.

Among the initial restoration projects was the replication of the Goddess of Liberty. Severely deteriorated and weakened by a century of exposure to the elements, the zinc statue was removed in November, 1985. A replica cast in aluminum was set in place with assistance of a helicopter.

Other work focused upon the grounds. In 1987 the Great Walk extending from the Eleventh Street entrance to the Capitol was relandscaped with young American elms, which replaced diseased elms planted in 1903. Soon thereafter drawings and specifications were prepared for the reconstruction of the walkway shaded by these trees.

Although a master plan has not yet been developed, plans are underway for the phased reconstruction of the office of the secretary of state, one of only two areas on the ground floor still used for its original function. The work is scheduled to include removal of fluorescent lighting and the acoustical ceiling, installation of reproduction chandeliers and of carpeting compatible with the room's historical appearance, and restoration of original wall, ceiling, and woodwork colors, hand-painted doors on the records vaults, woodwork, and hardware, all according to nationally accepted standards of restoration.[33] The governor's public reception room has been restored, thanks in part to a grant from the Heritage Society of Austin, and there has been interim restoration of the House of Representatives area.

Restoration planning and work in progress are certainly appropriate commemorations of the centennial of the construction of the Texas Capitol, the importance of which was recognized in 1986 when the Capitol was designated a National Historic Landmark, an honor reserved for America's most significant buildings.[34] Restoration should enhance both the sublime beauty and organic unity of the building,

---

[33] "Minutes," State Preservation Board, Jan. 25, 1988, p. 5 (Texas State Historical Commission, Austin).

[34] The National Historic Landmarks Program is administered by the National Park Service. At the time of the Capitol's designation there were 32 National Historic Landmarks in the State of Texas and about 1,700 in the country. *Medallion*, XXIII (Aug., 1986), 1.

which have been marred by unsympathetic treatment over the course of a century. It will certainly honor dedicated, farsighted Texas forefathers who had the vision to build an edifice that, a century later, still reflects their pride in the state and its representative government, and that will continue to impress countless generations to come.

"A Question of Great Delicacy": The Texas Capitol Competition, 1881

WILLIAM ELTON GREEN*

DESIGN COMPETITIONS IN THE UNITED STATES TO CHOOSE ARCHItects for public buildings took place as early as 1792, with competitions for the national Capitol and a house for the president. States and local governments also adopted the process and often utilized design competitions during the nineteenth and early twentieth centuries to obtain designs for capitols, college and university structures, courthouses, city halls, and other public buildings. Elected officials or appointed commissioners generally advertised for building designs and awarded a commission to draw plans for the proposed structure to the architect of the winning entry.[1]

The state of Texas held its first design competition in early 1852 to secure plans for a new Capitol in Austin. The competition attracted several entries, but the commissioners in charge—the governor, comptroller, and treasurer—allegedly "rejected all the plans submitted, *borowing* (?) [*sic*] enough from each to enable them to draft one of their own."[2] Controversies then developed over the construction of the new Capitol, including accusations of graft in the construction and furnishing of the building.[3] Nearly sixty years later, as Texas prepared to build a magnificent new structure to replace the old one, state officials determined to avoid the kind of mistakes that had been made in the 1850s. The same human weaknesses still existed, however, making the Texas design competition in 1881 "a question of great delicacy."[4]

---

*William Elton Green is the Capitol Historian for the State Preservation Board. He is the author of *The Dancing Was Lively; Fort Concho, Texas: A Social History, 1867 to 1882* (1974) and is currently writing a book on the Alamo, "Remembering the Alamo: The Development of a Texas Symbol, 1836–1986."

[1] Willard B. Robinson, *Texas Public Buildings of the Nineteenth Century* (Austin: University of Texas Press for Amon Carter Museum of Western Art, 1974), 203–206.

[2] *Texas Republican* (Marshall), Apr. 17, 1852.

[3] *Report of the Building and Furniture of the Capitol of the State of Texas* (Austin: Marshall & Oldham, State Printers, 1856).

[4] *Report of the Capitol Building Commissioners to the Governor of Texas, Austin, January 1, 1883* (Austin: E. W. Swindells, State Printer, 1883), 16.

   The Republic of Texas declared its independence at Washington-on-the-Brazos in 1836 but established no "permanent capital" until nearly three years later, when a special commission located the "City of Austin" on the north bank of the Colorado River between Waller and Shoal creeks.[5] The area on the city plat reserved as "Capitol Square" occupied the center and highest part of a horseshoe-shaped prominence in the north part of town, facing south down the city's main street, appropriately named "Congress Avenue." No doubt chosen because of its prominent location, the site for the future Capitol shows the practicality of the commissioners in choosing a spot safe from flooding and one cooled in summer by prevailing breezes from the southwest across the Colorado River.[6]

   The struggling Republic of Texas did not need and could not afford immediately to build a grand Capitol in 1839, so the government did as most settlers had done at first and erected a temporary wooden structure to house the Congress. The first Capitol stood southwest of Capitol Square, and several log buildings nearby served as offices for the president and other departments of the government. Fears resulting from the Mexican invasion of San Antonio in 1842 encouraged President Sam Houston to move the government back to the town of Houston, but Texas officials returned to Austin in late 1845, and the government continued to use the primitive structures built in 1839 after Texas became a state in 1846.[7] In 1846 a description of the 1839 Capitol appeared in a New England newspaper, possibly contributed by a Mexican War soldier:

The Texas "State House" or "Capitol" is a one story wooden building, made somewhat roughly inside and out, over 100 feet long, and 50 wide. . . . So far as comfort is concerned, no one suffers; and the Texians have no idea of LAVISHING money upon things to look at, just yet.[8]

   Not only did Texas have no desire to "lavish" money on a Capitol in 1846, but by the end of the Mexican War two years later the state had a

   [5] Map of "City of Austin and Vicinity," by W. H. Sandusky, draughtsman, 1839; Ernest William Winkler, "The Seat of Government of Texas," *Quarterly of the Texas State Historical Association*, X (Jan., 1907), 185–245. See especially, "Report of the Commissioners Named to Select a Permanent Capital for the Republic of Texas, City of Houston, April 13th A.D. 1839," Seat of Government Papers (Archives Division, Texas State Library, Austin), in Winkler, "Seat of Government," 217–220.
   [6] "Plan of the City of Austin," drawn by L. I. Pilie (1st and 2nd quotations) (New Orleans: Greene, Lithographer to the Republic of Texas, 1839).
   [7] O. M. Roberts, "The Capitals of Texas," *Quarterly of the Texas State Historical Association*, II (Oct., 1898), 119–120; Alex. W. Terrell, "The City of Austin from 1839 to 1865," ibid., XIV (Oct., 1910), 116–119.
   [8] *Herald* (Newburyport, Mass.), Oct. 29, 1846.

total debt amounting to $10,000,000. Partly as a result, in 1850 Texas agreed to give up its claims to a large disputed area northwest of the present state—including sections of present-day New Mexico, Oklahoma, Kansas, Colorado, and Wyoming—in exchange for $10,000,000 from the federal government. With the money, which eventually totaled about $12,750,000, Texas paid off its debts and then used the nearly $3,000,000 surplus to begin a permanent public school fund; construct a new Capitol, a governor's mansion, and a hospital for the insane; and operate the state government for several years without requiring any tax monies from the counties.[9]

Constructed in the Greek Revival style typical of many other public and private buildings at the time, three stories tall and about 140 feet long by 90 feet wide, the cream-colored limestone Capitol completed in 1853 stood on the site reserved as Capitol Square fourteen years earlier. Texans justifiably expressed pride in their new statehouse, and the well-known New York landscape architect Frederick Law Olmsted, on his trek across Texas in 1854, found the structure "a really imposing building."[10]

By the early 1870s, however, the structure had fallen into disrepair because the state possessed little money to maintain the building during the Civil War and its aftermath.[11] The legislature also probably hesitated to spend money repairing the Capitol because the 1869 constitution provided for another election to choose a "permanent seat" for the state government. In late 1872 Texas voters overwhelmingly approved a proposition to leave the capital at Austin and, for the first time since the Civil War, Democrats gained majorities in both the House and the Senate. Elections a year later returned to the Capitol a Democratic governor, Richard Coke. Early in 1874 the new legislature met and, with Coke's cooperation, began unraveling the acts of the Reconstruction period. One target was the 1869 constitution, a hated document that finally was replaced in 1876.[12]

Local newspapers commented occasionally about the poor condition of the Capitol and the need to repair it but they made no mention of

---

[9] Edmund Thornton Miller, *A Financial History of Texas*, Bulletin of the University of Texas, 1916, No. 37 (Austin, 1916), 86–89.

[10] August Watkins Harris, *Minor and Major Mansions in Early Austin: An Edition Composite* (Austin: n.p., 1958), n.p.; Frederick Law Olmsted, *A Journey through Texas; or, A Saddle-Trip on the Southwestern Frontier* (Austin: University of Texas Press, 1978), 110.

[11] During the Civil War the legislature approved an appropriation for repairing the roofs of "the Capitol, the General Land Office, the old Land Office and Treasury Buildings." See H. P. N. Gammel (comp.), *The Laws of Texas, 1882–1897* . . . (10 vols., Austin: Gammel Book Co., 1898), V, 616.

[12] Ibid., VII, 402 (quotation), 403, VIII, 396, 561; Alwyn Barr, *Reconstruction to Reform: Texas Politics, 1876–1906* (Austin: University of Texas Press, 1971), 8–9.

extensively renovating the old building or erecting a new one until the Democrats returned to control in 1874. By that time the growth of the state government from the 1850s to the 1870s had resulted in cramped conditions for officials and employees who occupied four buildings on Capitol Square: the Capitol and the General Land Office southeast of the Capitol, as well as a Supreme Court Building and a Treasurer and Comptroller's Building behind the Capitol.[13]

Taste had changed, too; as early as mid-1870 an article in *DeBow's Monthly Review* opined, "The Capitol is remarkably plain, with its three stories and simple square windows, as unpretending, save the graceful columns, as an ordinary cotton factory."[14] The construction of several new commercial and public buildings in Austin in the mid-1870s emphasized the shabbiness of the old Capitol. Thus, by the mid-1870s many Texans saw a need for extensive renovation or replacement of the old-fashioned, bat-infested limestone structure on Capitol Hill.

The First Session of the Fourteenth Legislature in 1874 passed an act to provide for care of the state buildings and cemetery. In November, 1874, Fred Voigt, the superintendent "in charge of the Capitol and other Public Property," submitted a report on the condition of the Capitol and other state buildings, the Capitol grounds, and the state cemetery, with an estimated cost of repairs needed after consulting "with practical mechanics and architects as to the best mode of repairing these buildings."[15] Of the Capitol, Voigt said:

This building is of ample dimensions and substantial material, but destitute of architectural proportions or beauty, and needs repairs to a considerable extent to secure its preservation, and these repairs should be of an ornamental as well as of a substantial character, which would materially change its present squatty and unsightly appearance.[16]

He also wrote,

The capitol is sufficiently capacious and durable to last for many years to come, should timely repairs be added, which pecuniarily will save the State perhaps a

---

[13] In 1850 the legislature provided for a General Land Office, constructed on the northwest part of Capitol Square prior to the building of the 1853 Capitol, and in 1853–1854 it appropriated money for a fireproof building for the treasurer and comptroller, erected on the northeast corner of Capitol Square. In 1856 the state built a new General Land Office on the southeast corner of the square and turned the old Land Office building into offices for staff of the governor, attorney general, and secretary of state. Finally, in 1871 the Supreme Court moved into the latter building. See Gammel (comp.), *Laws of Texas*, III, 787, 930–931, 1,325–1,326, 1,479, IV, 231–232, 236, VI, 978.

[14] "The City of Austin," *DeBow's Monthly Review*, VIII (July, 1870), 534.

[15] *Report of F. Voigt, in Charge of the Capitol and Other Public Property, for the Year 1874* (Houston: A. C. Gray, State Printer, 1874), 3 (2nd quotation).

[16] Ibid., 4 (3rd quotation).

million or more dollars in the near future, and a policy of economy would dictate a liberal provision of thorough repairs in every instance. It might be greatly improved, both in beauty and strength, by replacing the present unsightly covering with a mansard roof covered with slate, which improvement would furnish additional conveniences, render the building in a manner fire proof, and greatly improve its appearance.[17]

In his message to the legislature in January, 1875, Governor Coke encouraged lawmakers to provide the $33,000 requested by Voigt to repair the state buildings "and improve the grounds handsomely."[18] The governor added:

All the public buildings, except, perhaps, that which is used by the supreme court, are in a very dilapidated and unsafe condition, affording very insufficient protection to the valuable public archives and records, in all of them. The buildings, if properly repaired, will be preserved, and subserve the purpose for which they were built, many years yet, but uncared for, will soon become so much injured and dilapidated as to be unworthy of the state.[19]

In January the Austin *Daily Statesman* indicated that Joseph Sherwin, an English architect who recently had moved from Galveston to Austin, had drawn plans for a renovation of the Capitol "with a new front, Mansard roof and dome." The paper added, "If we cannot have an entirely new and modern Capitol building within the next few years, then we would like to see the present building improved, ornamented and relieved of its squatty and dilapidated appearance."[20]

Prior to moving to Austin, Sherwin had designed the new First Presbyterian Church completed there in early 1875. At the time, the Capital City had only one other architectural firm, Larmour and Wheelock. Soon after Sherwin's relocation, several Austin individuals and groups hired him to design residences, churches, and commercial structures. Hoping that the state would retain him to execute plans for a renovation of the Capitol, the English architect drew the proposed design on his own initiative, or possibly at Voigt's suggestion.[21]

---

[17] Ibid., 10.

[18] [*Journal of the House of Representatives of Texas, Being the Second Session of the Fourteenth Legislature, Begun and Held at the City of Austin, January 12, 1875* (Houston: A. C. Gray, State Printer, 1875)], 91–92. The title page is missing from the only copy of this volume that can be located, which is in the Archives Division, Texas State Library, Austin. The title utilized is based on the title of the Senate journal for the same session of the legislature.

[19] Ibid.

[20] Austin *Daily Statesman*, Jan. 10, 24 (quotations), 1875.

[21] Ibid., Nov. 13, 29, 1874, Jan. 27, Feb. 1 [Feb. 2], 9, Apr. 13, May 15, June 3, 13, July 6, 22, Aug. 1, 1875. Sherwin must have left Austin sometime during August, 1875, but the *Statesman* failed to mention his departure.

In late January the Austin *Daily Statesman* optimistically commented,

The drawing of the Capitol as it would appear should the Legislature see fit to make an appropriation for its improvement, as suggested in Mr. Voigt's report, is attracting considerable attention among the members and others.[22]

The newspaper reported that the proposed renovation would cost "about $25,000," but added:

It is a question worthy of some discussion, as to whether the improvements had better be made or the building used as it is for a few years and then a magnificent and costly one substituted for it. So far as we have been able to learn, the general drift of opinion among the heads of the departments and members is in favor of the improvements. The building is certainly large enough, and will be for years to come, and, whatever may be done, we hope the day is not distant when Texas will have a more imposing State House.[23]

The Second Session of the Fourteenth Legislature in 1875 made a $5,000 appropriation to landscape the Capitol grounds and passed a bill to light the Capitol with gas, but provided no other monies to repair or renovate the structure in spite of the proposition to do so, probably because of the lack of funds. The legislature also passed a joint resolution calling a convention to write a new constitution later in 1875.[24]

The Civil War, Reconstruction, and the nationwide panic of 1873 resulted in serious financial problems for Texas by 1875. The state's only wealth lay in its several million acres of public lands, located primarily in West Texas and the Panhandle—regions generally regarded as the least desirable for settlement or investment. Optimistically, however, the constitutional convention in late 1875 addressed the question of a new Capitol by setting aside more than three million acres of vacant land to finance its construction.[25]

Early in 1876 Texas voters approved the new constitution, and the Fifteenth Legislature—the first legislature to meet after adoption of the new charter—assembled later that year. In his report on public

[22] Ibid., Jan. 27, 1875.

[23] Ibid.

[24] *Journal of the Senate of Texas, Being the Second Session of the Fourteenth Legislature, Begun and Held at the City of Austin, January 12, 1875* (Houston: A. C. Gray, State Printer, 1875), 107, 111–112, 121, 127, 163, 169, 175, 180, 291, 303, 347, 583, 593, 607–608; *Journal of the House of Representatives . . . 1875*, pp. 91–92, 170, 194, 230, 233, 275, 301, 391; Texas, Fourteenth Legislature, *General Laws of the State of Texas . . . 1875* (Houston: A. C. Gray, State Printer, 1875), 24, 113, 189, 201–202.

[25] Aldon Socrates Lang, *Financial History of the Public Lands in Texas* (Waco: Baylor University, 1932); Thomas Lloyd Miller, *The Public Lands of Texas, 1519–1970* (Norman: University of Oklahoma Press, 1972), 59–125.

buildings for 1875, Fred Voigt again called attention to the poor condition of the old Capitol and added pessimistically,

It would seem exceedingly doubtful whether a sufficient amount of money could be realized from the sale of land set aside for that purpose to warrant the building of a new Capitol (such as shall be in keeping with the greatness of the State) in the near future; and I, therefore, beg to recommend an appropriation adequate to improve the building in a thorough and substantial manner, which will then serve its purpose for many years to come.[26]

The legislature failed to approve such an appropriation, however, and also declined to provide for surveying of the Capitol lands.[27]

Under the new constitution the Sixteenth Legislature did not meet until nearly three years later, but local newspapers continued to promote construction of a new Capitol. For example, one writer in 1877 observed:

[The] Capitol buildings are sadly out of keeping with a progressive city and prosperous State. This is the more noticeable now that a magnificent court house graces the Avenue within sight of the Capitol grounds. The next legislature should make an ample appropriation for the erection of a capitol building in keeping with the tastes of the citizens of a great and prosperous State.[28]

In the meantime Texas voters elected as governor Oran M. Roberts, who took office in 1879, shortly before the new legislature convened. Elected on a platform of retrenchment and dedicated to lowering Texas's public debt, Roberts subscribed to a "pay as you go" policy that resulted in reducing pensions to Texas veterans and decreased appropriations to Texas public schools.[29] The conservative-minded Roberts

---

[26] *Report of F. Voigt, in Charge of the Capitol and Other Public Property . . . for the Year 1875* (Austin: Institution for the Deaf and Dumb, 1876), 4.

[27] *Journal of the Senate of Texas, Being the First Session of the Fifteenth Legislature, Begun and Held at the City of Austin, April 18, 1876* (Galveston: Shaw & Blaylock, State Printers, 1876), 153, 246–247, 440; *Journal of the House of Representatives of the State of Texas, First Session of the Fifteenth Legislature, Begun and Held at the City of Austin, April 18, 1876* (Galveston: Shaw & Blaylock, State Printers, 1876), 220, 308–309, 857, 908, 931, 952, 988, 990.

[28] Austin *Daily Statesman*, Mar. 25, 1877.

[29] Born in South Carolina, Roberts graduated from the University of Alabama in 1836 and then studied law. Admitted to the bar in 1837, he served one term in the Alabama legislature before coming to Texas in 1841. Roberts settled in St. Augustine, where he served as district attorney and district judge and taught law at the University of St. Augustine. In early 1857 he became an associate justice of the Texas Supreme Court. A strong secessionist, in January, 1861, Roberts played an important role in calling the Secession Convention and served as its president. During the Civil War he commanded a regiment of Texas infantry, until becoming chief justice of the state supreme court in 1864.

Although he was removed from the court after the Civil War, Roberts helped write the Texas Constitution of 1866 and was elected to the United States Senate, but was denied a seat there because of his participation in secession. With the return of Democratic rule in Texas in 1874,

also may have wished only "to patch up" the old Capitol instead of building a new one, but he signed two bills passed by the legislature in 1879 that provided for surveying the Capitol lands in ten counties of the Texas Panhandle and for building a new state Capitol.[30]

Probably as a result of the problems suffered by the state relating to construction of the 1853 Capitol, the two acts created a Capitol Board and a Building Commission with a superintendent to oversee construction. Composed of the state's elected executive officials—governor, comptroller, treasurer, attorney general—and the commissioner of the General Land Office, the Capitol Board had the responsibility of appointing a commissioner to supervise surveying of the Capitol lands, as well as two building commissioners and "a skillful . . . architect" as building superintendent.[31]

The Capitol Board could not announce a design competition until completion of the land surveys, but passage of the law providing for construction of the Texas Capitol attracted the immediate attention of architects. In July, 1879, the Austin *Daily Statesman* indicated that Austin architect James Wahrenberger and his partner John W. Glenn had drawn plans for a new three-story Capitol "255 feet square and 247 feet to the summit of the dome, the edifice covering an area of 65,025 square feet, and the whole to cost $1,773,640."[32] The paper made no further mention of the plan, but Wahrenberger may have entered the same design in the Capitol competition in early 1881.

Architects in other parts of the country also expressed a premature interest in designing the new Texas Capitol. In late August the Austin *Daily Statesman* claimed:

Mr. [Alfred B.] Mullett, ex-Supervising Architect of the Treasury, is preparing plans and specifications for the construction of the Capitol. So are Brown & Jones, famous architects of St. Louis, and James B. Cook [an English-born architect in Memphis, Tennessee], the latter a student of Humboldt.[33]

Roberts became chief justice of the supreme court again and served in that capacity until his election as governor in late 1878 and 1880. In 1883 Roberts became professor of law at the newly established University of Texas, retiring in 1893. See Lelia Bailey, "The Life and Public Career of O. M. Roberts, 1815–1883" (Ph.D. diss., University of Texas, 1932).

[30] The Galveston *Daily News* claimed in an 1881 editorial, "The first idea of Gov. Roberts was, it has been understood, to patch up the old structure." See Galveston *Daily News*, Jan. 5, 1881; Gammel (comp.), *Laws of Texas*, VIII, 1,309–1,311, 1,411–1,415.

[31] Gammel (comp.), *Laws of Texas*, VIII, 1,309–1,311, 1,411–1,415, IX, 219 (quotation).

[32] Austin *Daily Statesman*, July 27, 1879.

[33] Ibid., Aug. 28, 1879. For Mullett see Henry F. Withey and Elsie Rathburn Withey, *Biographical Dictionary of American Architects (Deceased)* (Los Angeles: New Age Publishing Co., 1956), 432. The firm of "Brown & Jones" is not yet identified. For Cook see ibid., 135. For additional information on James B. Cook see James Patrick, *Architecture in Tennessee, 1768–1897* (Knoxville: University of Tennessee Press, 1981), 39, 145, 157, 183, 184, 209.

In September the newspaper announced that "one of the most famous architects in the United States, in a private letter to a gentleman of this city," had written:

I have not been able to find out anything in regard to the construction of your State Capitol. There is nothing stated of its size, kind or cost. If I can get the needful information I will prepare plans; but I greatly fear that in Texas, as elsewhere in such cases, the proposition to have a fair competition is a delusion and a snare. The architect and contractors are already staked out and the corrupt are always incompetent. . . . Is it too late?[34]

Elijah E. Myers of Detroit, who ultimately became the architect for the new Texas Capitol, also wrote Governor Roberts on September 8, 1879, saying:

I am informed that your state authorities contemplate erecting a Capitol Building and I would respectively ask permission to submit plans for the proposed building. I furnished the plans for the Michigan State Capitol and superintended its erection. Should you desire plans for any of your Public Buildings, I will most cheerfully furnish them at reasonable rates.[35]

Later in the month Myers sent Roberts several photographs of his work, including views of the Michigan Capitol and of "the New Asylum for the Insane at Pontiac, Michigan."[36]

During September Governor Roberts also received an inquiry from A. G. Whittlesey of Evansville, Indiana, saying:

I have learned that some preliminary action has been taken in Your State, looking to the erection of a new State House, but have no information as to the progress made in that direction. Being a civil engineer by profession and connected with one of the best architects and builders associations in the West I take the liberty of inquiring of Your Excellency whether my information (with respect to the intention of Your State and legislative authorities to erect a new Capitol building) is correct. If so be good enough to inform me whether a design for the proposed edifice has been selected, or whether any steps have been taken in the matter and to what extent. If practicable our association would be glad to enter into the Competition for the furnishing of plans and advancing the work. The fullest information you can give in the premises will be thankfully received. If there is a prospect for business I would be pleased to visit your young, vigorous and very remarkable State.

It may not be amiss, in the connection, to say that I was Secretary for Governor Thomas A. Hendricks during his incumbency of the Gubernatorial Office

[34] Austin *Daily Statesman*, Sept. 7, 1879.

[35] Elijah E. Myers to Oran M. Roberts, Sept. 8, 1879, Governors' Papers: O. M. Roberts (Archives Division, Texas State Library, Austin).

[36] Myers to Roberts, Sept. 20, 1879, ibid.

in Indiana, and I can refer with pleasure, to him for information respecting my character, fitness, etc.[37]

Roberts soon replied through his secretary, and Whittlesey wrote again in late September:

Referring to your letter to me of the 15th inst., written by Your private secretary, I have to ask a little further information concerning Your proposed new Capitol for which I shall be exceedingly obliged.

Has Your Legislature (or other Competent authority) fixed a time within which competitive designs shall be presented for examination? If so what is the date?

What persons have been authorized to receive and pass upon the merits of such designs? Have any specific instructions been issued for the Government of architects? If such instructions have been issued and the same are published I should be pleased to receive a copy.[38]

In July, 1879, Governor Roberts appointed Nimrod Lindsay Norton of Salado as commissioner to supervise surveying of the Capitol lands. A native of Kentucky, Norton attended schools in New York and Kentucky before moving in the 1850s to Missouri, where he organized one of the first Confederate companies in the state and later became a representative to the Confederate Congress. After the war Norton settled with his family at Salado, Texas, and in 1873 he helped organize the Grange, a conservative farmers' organization that in 1875 exerted much influence on the writing of the new Texas constitution. Roberts probably knew Norton in connection with the Grange.[39]

The survey of the Capitol lands began in 1879; in September, 1880, Norton gave the surveying notes and a report on the lands to the Capitol Board, which sent the material to the General Land Office for verification. Afterward, the governor and comptroller had the responsibility of estimating the value of the lands. Such details undoubtedly consumed a great deal of time, but Governor Roberts also probably did not want to do anything that would upset his reelection in early November, 1880. The Capitol Board, therefore, did not meet to accept the survey and estimate until mid-November.[40]

After accepting the report on the Capitol lands, the board appointed Norton and Joseph Lee on November 16 as Capitol building commis-

---

[37] A. G. Whittlesey to Roberts, Sept. 11, 1879, ibid.

[38] Whittlesey to Roberts, Sept. 23, 1879, ibid.

[39] John Henry Brown, *Indian Wars and Pioneers of Texas* (Austin: L. E. Daniell, [189?]), 697–700; Clement A. Evans (ed.), *Confederate Military History* (12 vols.; Atlanta: Confederate Publishing Co., 1899), XI, 564–566.

[40] *Report of the Capitol Building Commissioners* (1883), 4–8.

THE NEW CAPITOL OF TEXAS.

This steel engraving, 4½ × 9 inches, shows the Texas Capitol as initially designed by Elijah E. Myers. Notice the square tower which the Capitol board asked Myers to change to a dome. From the Austin *Weekly Statesman,* December 16, 1886. *Courtesy Barker Texas History Center, The University of Texas at Austin.*

sioners. Nothing indicates that either of the commissioners had any particular knowledge of architecture, and both undoubtedly received their appointments chiefly for political reasons. The fifty-year-old Norton probably received his appointment because the Capitol Board approved the manner in which he had discharged his responsibilities in supervising the survey of the Capitol lands.[41]

Twenty years older than Norton, born and educated in Ohio, Joseph Lee studied law before moving to Texas in 1840 and settling in Austin. In 1841 he was appointed chief justice of Travis County by President Mirabeau B. Lamar, and in 1842 he helped lead Austin residents in the so-called Archives War, which succeeded in preventing the government from moving the archives to Houston. Elected to the Texas House of Representatives in 1857, Lee played an active role in the state Democratic party for many years. He undoubtedly was familiar with the problems encountered in construction of the 1853 Capitol. His appointment may have owed much to his widespread reputation for honesty and conscientiousness, but it probably amounted chiefly to pensioning an elderly statesman.[42]

[41] Ibid., 13.

[42] William S. Speer and John Henry Brown (eds.), *The Encyclopedia of the New West* (Marshall, Tex.: United States Biographical Publishing Co., 1881), 418–419; *Biographical Souvenir of the State of Texas . . .* (Chicago: F. A. Battey & Co., 1889), 513–514.

On November 17, the day after appointing the two commissioners and probably after discussing the matter with them, the Capitol Board hired Austin architect Jasper N. Preston as superintendent for construction of the Capitol. A native of New York, Preston (1832–189?) studied architecture and worked as a draftsman in Lansing, Michigan, in the early 1870s. He undoubtedly knew Elijah E. Myers, who won the competition to design the Texas Capitol, because Myers also lived in Lansing in the early 1870s while supervising construction of the Michigan Capitol, which he designed.[43]

After moving to Austin in 1875, Preston became locally prominent as an architect and practiced briefly with Frederick Ernst Ruffini soon after the latter's arrival in 1877. Alone and in partnership with Ruffini, Preston designed a number of commercial buildings and other projects in Austin. He "filled the position of architect to the state for asylums" and designed an addition to the Lunatic Asylum at Austin in 1878. Thus, he probably met and knew many people in state government who supported his appointment as superintendent.[44]

---

[43] Withey and Withey, *Biographical Dictionary of American Architects*, 486. Interestingly, the Austin *Daily Statesman*, Nov. 7, 1881, noted:

E. E. Myers, architect of the new capitol, left the city [Austin] yesterday for his home, in Michigan. He was accompanied by Mr. Preston, architect of this city, and Capt. W. M. Wilson, president of the board of trustees of the state lunatic asylum. The object of the visit north of the latter gentlemen is, doubtless, to examine the architecture and construction of public buildings there, having in view the additions to be made to the insane asylum.

According to a letter from Myers to Governor Roberts four months later, submitting proposed designs for the first University of Texas building, Myers said he had "furnished the plans . . . for the new wings of the [Texas] asylum for the insane." Myers to Roberts, Mar. 7, 1882, O. M. Roberts Papers (Eugene C. Barker Texas History Center, University of Texas at Austin).

[44] Preston's notable works in Austin include the Tips Building (1876), the Hannig Building (1876), and a renovation of the old First Baptist Church (1880), directly across Colorado Street from the Governor's Mansion. Immediately prior to his appointment as capitol superintendent, Preston designed a structure for Tillotson Institute (1881), a newly established school for black students in Austin. Later in 1881 he worked in partnership with Austin architect James Wahrenberger, and in 1883 he established a partnership with his son, Samuel A. J. Preston, who managed a branch office in San Antonio.

Preston designed the Cameron County Courthouse (1882) in Brownsville, Texas, the Bastrop County Courthouse (1883) in Bastrop, Texas, and possibly the Mitchell County Courthouse (1884) in Colorado City, Texas. In partnership with his son, Preston later designed the Bell County Courthouse (1884) in Belton, Texas—the tower and entrances of which originally bore a striking similarity to the square dome and north entrance of the competition drawings for the Texas Capitol by Myers, as well as to his plans for the Arapahoe (later Denver) County, Colorado, Courthouse (1883). The Prestons also designed Austin's Driskill Hotel (1886). Both Prestons became charter members of the Texas State Association of Architects, organized in Austin in 1886, but later that year the men moved to Los Angeles, California. Elected president of the Southern California Chapter of the American Institute of Architects in 1892, Jasper N. Preston continued to practice architecture until at least 1896. Withey and Withey, *Biographical Dictionary of American Architects*, 486–487. See also, Austin *Daily Statesman*, Oct. 27, 1875, Mar. 19, May 12, 1876, Feb. 9, Feb. 15, Sept. 16, 1877, May 7, 1878, Mar. 14, 1880, July 7, Aug. 12, Nov. 6, 1881, Jan. 4, 1882, Jan. 5, 1883, Nov. 27, 1885, Dec. 17, 1886; San Antonio *Daily Express*, Jan. 10, 1883.

Less than a week after the board hired them, the two commissioners and the superintendent completed a description of the proposed new Capitol for use in soliciting plans and specifications as required by the 1879 act. Surprisingly, the three men visited no other state capitols in preparation. Architect Jasper N. Preston probably wrote most of the *Notice to Architects* because of his knowledge of architecture in general and the Michigan Capitol in particular. Preston also may have received help in writing the description from other architects in Austin, including former partner Frederick Ernst Ruffini and future partner James Wahrenberger—both of whom entered designs in the Capitol competition.[45]

The *Notice to Architects* specified how many rooms would be required for various officials; it also stipulated that the legislative chambers be located on the second floor and courtrooms on the third floor. In addition, the description required that the Capitol be built of stone, that the structure face south in the center of Capitol Square, and that it cost $1,500,000. The notice also included guidelines for lighting, heating, ventilation, and acoustics, and stipulated that "the building must be made as nearly as possible fire-proof."[46]

The 1880 census listed fifty-two architects in Texas, but none of these men had achieved much prominence outside of Texas or their native states. Wishing to obtain the best design possible, the Capitol building commissioners advertised nationally for plans for the new Capitol. The commissioners offered the paltry sum of $1,700 for the winning entry and no prizes for second and third choices, a decision that revealed their naivete about architectural fees and reflected, at the same time, the conservative view toward government spending held by Governor Roberts and most other Texans, together with large numbers of southerners.[47]

The Galveston *Daily News* particularly criticized the short time given architects to prepare plans for the Capitol competition: only two months from the publication of the *Notice to Architects* until the deadline of February 1, 1881. In fact, the short time allotted seemed to prejudice the competition in favor of architects who might have heard of it ahead of time, including those living in Austin, like Ruffini and Wahrenberger,

[45] *Report of the Capitol Building Commissioners* (1883), 14–15.

[46] Ibid.

[47] U.S., Department of the Interior, Census Office, *Statistics of the Population of the United States at the Tenth Census (June 1, 1880)* . . . (Washington, D.C., Government Printing Office, 1883), 768–769. The total number of architects in Texas reported in the 1880 census may not include an architect admitted to the Texas Penitentiary at Huntsville between 1870 and October 31, 1880. *Biennial Reports of the Directors and Superintendent of the Texas State Penitentiary at Huntsville, Texas, with the Report of the Prison Physician, Commencing 1, A.D. 1878, and Terminating October 31, A.D. 1880* (Galveston: The News Book and Job Office, 1881), 63.

and W. K. Dobson in San Antonio. Preston also may have informed Elijah E. Myers. As a result, some of the architects who entered designs probably had much longer to prepare competition plans than others.[48]

Several newspapers criticized the meager prize offered for the winning design and the lack of prizes for the second- and third-place entries. The Galveston *Daily News* believed the premium so "wholly inadequate" that the contest would not attract any "really first-class architects."[49] The newspaper also believed that the competition should have extended until June 1, 1881, and that prizes of $3,000, $2,000, and $1,000 should have been awarded for the three best plans, adding:

Texas is able and willing to pay a first-class price, and the people expect the Legislature to see to it that the State—the State whole and indivisible—gets a first-class capitol, and that no botch work of any kind is inflicted upon the Austin landscape and posterity.[50]

Not surprisingly, the competition only attracted eleven sets of plans by eight different architects, none of whom enjoyed national recognition. Four of the architects lived outside of Texas, including Elijah E. Myers of Detroit, John Andrewartha of Louisville, Mathias Harvey Baldwin of Memphis, and the sole woman who entered the contest—a mysterious and still unidentified "Mrs. Banting" of Burlington, Iowa. Probably because of the niggardly prize offered, several of the best-known architects in Texas did not enter plans. These included Alfred Giles of San Antonio, Nicholas J. Clayton of Galveston, Eugene T. Heiner of Houston, Wesley C. Dodson and William E. Larmour of Waco, James E. Flanders of Dallas, and Jacob L. Larmour and Jasper N. Preston of Austin.[51]

Two of the four Texas architects who drew plans for the Capitol competition lived in Austin in 1880: James Wahrenberger and Frederick

---

[48] Galveston *Daily News*, Jan. 5, Feb. 24, 1881.

[49] Ibid., Jan. 5, 1881.

[50] Ibid.

[51] Austin *Daily Statesman*, Apr. 30, 1881; *Report of the Capitol Building Commissioners* (1883), 15. Research efforts to identify "Mrs. Banting" have failed thus far. For information on architects working in Texas during the period, see Drury Blakeley Alexander, *Texas Homes of the Nineteenth Century* (Austin: University of Texas Press for Amon Carter Museum of Western Art, 1966); and three books by Willard B. Robinson: *Texas Public Buildings of the Nineteenth Century; Gone from Texas: Our Lost Architectural Heritage* (College Station, Tex.: Texas A&M University Press, 1981); *The People's Architecture: Texas Courthouses, Jails, and Municipal Buildings* (Austin: Texas State Historical Association in cooperation with the Center for Studies in Texas History, University of Texas at Austin, 1983). See also, Howard Barnstone, *The Galveston That Was* (New York: Macmillan Co., 1966); Mary Carolyn Hollers Jutson, *Alfred Giles: An English Architect in Texas and Mexico* (San Antonio: Trinity University Press, 1972); and Roxanne Kuter Williamson, *Austin, Texas: An American Architectural History* (San Antonio: Trinity University Press, 1973).

Ernst Ruffini. The only Texas-born Architect entering the competition and probably the youngest to submit plans, James Wahrenberger (1855–1929) ironically possessed more formal architectural training than some of the others, though he had less practical experience. Born of Swiss parents in Austin in 1855, Wahrenberger attended preparatory school in Philadelphia and in 1872 went to Europe, where he studied architecture for five years in Germany and Switzerland. He also traveled extensively in Europe before returning in 1878 to Austin, where he entered a partnership with John Glenn.[52]

By 1880 Wahrenberger had become a partner of Jacob Larmour (1822–1901), a New Jersey native who had worked as an architect first in New York City and later in Mississippi, Indiana, and Minnesota. In 1871 Larmour came to Austin, where he became extremely prominent during the 1870s, designing several homes and commercial buildings as well as the Travis County Courthouse (1875). Governor Roberts appointed Larmour state architect in 1879, probably to inspect state penitentiaries, but for unexplained reasons Larmour did not enter plans in the Capitol competition.[53]

Born in Cleveland, Ohio, Frederick Ernst Ruffini (1851–1885) studied architecture in New York and Boston and worked for architectural firms in both cities. He later worked in Cleveland, Cincinnati, Chicago, Indianapolis, and Louisville. According to the Austin *Daily Statesman*, Ruffini's design for the courthouse and city hall at Chicago, Illinois, was awarded a first premium of $5,000 over fifty-three competitors. Ruffini claimed to have entered a design in the Indiana Capitol competition and to have "assisted in preparing the preliminary sketches" for the new Indiana Capitol, evidently in the employ of another architect.[54]

Ruffini moved to Austin in early 1877 and soon became the partner of Jasper N. Preston, who had arrived in town only two years earlier. During the next three years Ruffini designed some commercial buildings and residences in Austin, as well as several Texas courthouses. In

---

[52] *Memorial and Genealogical Record of Southwest Texas* (Chicago: Goodspeed Brothers, Publishers, 1894), 561–562; San Antonio *Express*, Oct. 23, 1928; Austin *Daily Statesman*, July 27, 1879, Mar. 17, 1880; San Antonio *Evening Light*, Sept. 28, Nov. 15, 1882; *C. D. Morrison & Co.'s General Directory of the City of Austin, for 1879–80* (Marshall, Tex.: Jennings Bros., 1879), 84, 177, 192; *San Antonio, Texas* (St. Louis: Geo. W. Engelhardt & Co., Publishers, [1891]), 60; J. S. Reilly, *San Antonio, Past Present & Future . . .* (San Antonio: J. S. Reilly, [1885]), 127–128; Withey and Withey, *Biographical Dictionary of American Architects*, 622.

[53] Austin *Daily Statesman*, May 3, 1879, Mar. 17, 1880; Sally S. Victor, "Jacob Larmour," unpublished manuscript in biographical vertical files (Austin History Center, Austin Public Library).

[54] F. E. and Oscar Ruffini Papers (Archives Division, Texas State Library, Austin); Austin *Daily Statesman*, Feb. 13, 1881 (quotation).

December, 1880, shortly after publication of the Texas Capitol competition, Ruffini visited the newly erected capitols in Illinois, Iowa, and Michigan, as well as those in Ohio, Tennessee, and the Capitol under construction in Indiana.[55] The Austin *Daily Statesman* said:

The information gained will be fully embodied into the designs Mr. Ruffini is preparing for our new Capitol, and this, coupled with the practical knowledge of our state's resources, obtained by the successful erection of some eight or ten court houses and other public buildings in our state, will fairly place Mr. Ruffini's plans on an equal, if not superior, footing with any foreign designs that may be sent here.[56]

Ruffini submitted two plans for the Texas Capitol, but one of these may have been his unsuccessful entry in the Indiana competition. The Austin *Daily Statesman* published two articles in early 1881 that clearly favored one of Ruffini's designs. This entry, labeled "San Jacinto," was the only design that the newspaper commented about in any detail.[57]

The paper said that Ruffini had submitted a design for a fireproof building with every room "lighted and ventilated from the exterior." The proposed structure featured two large courtyards and three domes: a large one over the rotunda and smaller ones over each wing. The Renaissance Revival design included statues at the main entrance of "leading statesmen or renowned personages," as well as the state seal, and "the names of the leading battles for independence."[58]

W. K. Dobson, who had moved to San Antonio from Nashville, Tennessee, in 1879, also entered the Capitol competition. The Austin *Daily Statesman* noted on December 10, 1880, that Dobson "was in the city examining the grounds with a view of drawing a plan for a statehouse. He comes highly recommended as an architect of great skill and experience."[59] Dobson appeared in Nashville directories as early as 1855 as a "carver" and submitted carvings at various exhibitions there from 1855 to 1857. He entered a partnership with another architect in the late

---

[55] Austin *Daily Statesman*, Feb. 9, Feb. 15, 1877, Dec. 19, 1880. Ruffini designed a number of structures in Austin, including the Millett Opera House (1878) and the Hancock Building (1880). He designed courthouses in Rusk County (1879), Gregg County (1879), Navarro County (1881), Hopkins County (1882), Hays County (1882), Williamson County (ca. 1882), Blanco County (1885), and Concho County (1885). F. E. Ruffini also designed the first building at the University of Texas (1882). Robinson, *The People's Architecture*, 63, 72 n., 80, 103, 108, 113, 116, 117, 118; Williamson, *Austin, Texas*, 82–83.

[56] Austin *Daily Statesman*, Dec. 19, 1880.

[57] Ibid., Feb. 13, Mar. 13, 1881. In 1883 Ruffini entered two sets of plans in the first Colorado Capitol competition, but Colorado refused to accept any of the designs and held another contest in 1885. Myers also entered the first Colorado competition in 1883.

[58] Austin *Daily Statesman*, March 13, 1881.

[59] Austin *Daily Statesman*, Dec. 10, 1880.

1860s and designed a number of homes and churches in Nashville and middle Tennessee during the 1870s. After moving to San Antonio, Dobson designed several commercial structures and homes there.[60] No description of Dobson's design appeared in the Austin or San Antonio newspapers, but the San Antonio *Daily Express* commented: "Dobson's plans for the state capitol are not as gaudily polished as the designs of some others, but it is really believed that it will be adopted. Its novelty and originality are very much admired."[61]

William Otto Glosnop of Clarksville also entered a design in the Capitol competition. A talented German-born cabinetmaker, Glosnop designed some houses in Clarksville, where he probably lived from the 1860s until his death in 1895, but little other information survives concerning him. A table with a marquetry top crafted by Glosnop received an award for the "Best Center Table" at the Third Annual Exposition in Austin in November, 1877. Several other pieces of furniture made by Glosnop and at least two surviving houses designed by him suggest that he was a better cabinetmaker than architect.[62]

English-born John Andrewartha (1839–1916), who became a Texas resident in early 1881, had come to the United States just after the Civil War and settled in Louisville, Kentucky. He probably knew Ruffini, who also resided in Louisville in the mid-1870s, and may even have worked with him. Andrewartha designed a number of commercial

---

[60] Joseph L. Herndon, "Architects in Tennessee until 1930: A Dictionary" (M.S. thesis, Columbia University, 1975), 59; Patrick, *Architecture in Tennessee*, 181, 189, 200–202. According to the San Antonio newspapers, Dobson received appointment as architect of the Sandwich Islands in late 1882 and left Texas. Nothing else is known of his career. The staff at the Hawaii State Archives did not locate any information about Dobson in their records. Janet Azama to W. E. G., Oct. 21, 1987, File: "Dobson, W. K.," in files of the Capitol Historian, Office of the Architect of the [Texas] Capitol, State Preservation Board (these files will eventually be deposited in the Archives Division, Texas State Library). See also San Antonio *Daily Express*, Nov. 7, 1879, Aug. 18, 1881, May 21, June 21, 1882, San Antonio *Evening Light*, July 28, 1881, Sept. 28, Nov. 15, Dec. 1, 1882. James Riely Gordon, a Virginia-born architect who came to Texas in 1887 and set up a practice in San Antonio, claimed in 1931 that he was "associated" in the mid-1880s in the East with a "W. K. Dobson, an eminent specialist in public buildings." Gordon continued, "During and since his gradual retirement I continued as a specialist in this particular field of architecture." James Riely Gordon to Board of Capitol Commissioners, State of North Dakota, June 22, 1931, James Riely Gordon Papers (Architectural Drawings Collection, University of Texas at Austin).

[61] San Antonio *Daily Express*, Apr. 22, 1881, reprinted in Austin *Daily Statesman*, Apr. 26, 1881.

[62] In spite of his long residence in Clarksville, little information survives about Glosnop. William Hill of Houston, Texas, reputedly owns the table made by Glosnop. See Salle Stemmons to Ann Alcorn, Dec. 19, 1985 (with copy of the certificate given Glosnop for the "Best Center Table" enclosed), File: "Glosnop, William O."; Roy Eugene Graham to Mrs. William P. Clements, Jr., Apr. 14, 1987, ibid.; Clements to William Hill, Apr. 29,1987, ibid.; Mrs. Bill Hale to W. E. G., Jan. 21, 1988, ibid. Mrs. Hale owns a mantlepiece made by Glosnop, and several other pieces of furniture made by him survive in Clarksville homes. One of the houses reputedly designed and built by Glosnop is at 407 East Main Street in Clarksville. See Alexander, *Texas Homes of the Nineteenth Century*, 199, 267.

buildings, schools, an addition to the state penitentiary, and a "lunatic asylum," as well as the Louisville City Hall (1873). Although his 1869 entry in the Kentucky Capitol competition was rejected, the Louisville *Ledger* claimed four years later that "his designs for the State Capitol, although not adopted on account of their magnificent proportions, being considered too much in advance at that time, are still considered the only plans upon which such a building should have been built." The unsuccessful Kentucky entry may have been one of the three sets of plans that Andrewartha entered in the Texas competition.[63]

Born in Philadelphia, Elijah E. Myers (1832–1909) gave up the study of law to become a carpenter and joiner and also studied architecture. In 1863 he moved to Springfield, Illinois, where he advertised as a "Practical Architect" and designed several Illinois courthouses during the late 1860s. Myers moved to Detroit in 1871 and won the Michigan Capitol design competition in early 1872. He supervised construction of the building at Lansing from 1872 to 1879 and resided there temporarily during that period. In addition, Myers designed the Pontiac State Hospital at Pontiac, Michigan, and a number of courthouses, city halls, and churches in several states, as well as some private dwellings.[64]

Mathias Harvey Baldwin (1827–1891), a New York architect, moved to Memphis in 1859 and became one of the architects who "revolutionized design in Tennessee" after the Civil War. Baldwin designed a number of homes and commercial buildings in Memphis.[65]

The Capitol Board immediately placed the competing plans on public exhibit in the Supreme Courtroom, and the Austin *Daily Statesman* thought that "out of these the plan for a capitol, commensurate with requirements, can certainly be selected."[66] On the other hand, the more cosmopolitan Galveston *Daily News* criticized the display of the competition plans because it feared the public would favor certain

---

[63] Lousiville *Daily Ledger,* Sept. 18, 1873. Henry Russell Hitchcock and William Seale, *Temples of Democracy: The State Capitols of the USA* (New York: Harcourt Brace Javonovich, 1976), 250. Soon after arriving in Austin in 1877 Ruffini claimed he had designed "the new *Courier-Journal* block at Louisville, one of the finest newspaper buildings in the country." See Austin *Daily Statesman,* Feb. 15, 1877. On the other hand, information compiled by the Louisville Landmarks Commission indicates that Andrewartha won a design competition to build the structure in 1874.

[64] Myers's ad appeared in the *Illinois State Journal* (Springfield), Jan. 24, 1864, and is quoted in Martha Ann Kuepper Koellner, "Elijah E. Myers (1832–1909), Architect" (M.A. thesis, Western Illinois University, 1972), 2. See also Marlene Elizabeth Heck, "The Practice of E. E. Myers" (M.A. thesis, University of Virginia, 1977); *Cyclopedia of Michigan: Historical and Biographical* (New York: Western Publishing Co., n.d.), 314–315.

[65] Patrick, *Architecture in Tennessee,* 29, 183, 184 (quotation), 188, 189, 197, 198, 242; Barbara Flanary to W. E. G., Nov. 10, 1987, File: "Baldwin, Mathias," in files of the Capitol Historian.

[66] Austin *Daily Statesman,* Feb. 3, 1881.

Texas State Capitol Building by Elijah E. Myers, 1882. Watercolor, 41 × 64 inches. This black and white copy of the colorful Myers rendering on the cover contains the entire image of the painting.

plans over others and possibly pressure the board to accept an inferior design. The newspaper also suggested that the Capitol Board

ask the Legislature to increase the premium for the best plan to at least $5000, and permit those already submitted to be withdrawn for such changes and improvements as may be suggested by closer scrutiny, reopening competition, in fact, upon a more liberal scale and confining the selection to competent persons exempted from all influences.[67]

In late February and March, 1881, the Austin *Daily Statesman* published several articles by an unidentified correspondent knowledgeable about architectural history and current trends—probably a local architect—who discussed the competition generally and suggested ways of analyzing the plans entered. The author indicated that several of the designs had been entered in previous Capitol competitions. According to the articles, most of the designs in the competition utilized the Renaissance Revival style popular at the time. The writer opined, "A mistake may be made in the selection of the most suitable plan, but certainly out of four or five designs a mistake can not possibly be made in the selection of a beautiful one."[68] Interestingly, the last article in the

---

[67] Galveston *Daily News*, Feb. 24, 1881; see also paraphrase of the *News* editorial in San Antonio *Evening Light*, Feb. 26, 1881.

[68] Austin *Daily Statesman*, Feb. 26 (quotation), Mar. 1, 3, 6, 11, 13, 1881.

series paid particular attention to one of the plans submitted by Ruffini under the designation of "San Jacinto" and urged its selection.[69]

The Capitol Board realized its lack of experience to chose the best design from the eleven entries, and undoubtedly also wished to avoid charges of favoritism as well as personal problems—especially with the three architects living in Austin who had submitted designs. As a result, in response to a request from Governor Roberts, the legislature in mid-February passed a joint resolution providing $2,000 to hire "a skilled and impartial architect, or architects" to make the final decision. The resolution described the selection of a plan for the Capitol as "a question of great delicacy" that "necessarily involves great responsibility to the end that satisfaction may be assured."[70]

After seeking the advice of Texas representative Roger Q. Mills in Washington, D.C., the Capitol Board requested prominent New York Architect Napoléon Le Brun to come to Austin and choose the plan for the Texas Capitol. One of the best-known architects in the United States in 1881 and a fellow of the American Institute of Architects, Le Brun had designed a number of important structures in Philadelphia and New York. The New York architect refused to come to Texas for less than $3,000, in addition to his traveling expenses—a fee nearly twice the amount offered by the board to the competition winner and $1,000 (plus the traveling expenses) more than the joint resolution of the legislature appropriated. But the board hired Le Brun anyway, indicating how strongly it realized the need for help in choosing the Capitol plan and how much confidence it placed in his ability to make the selection.[71]

In the meantime the Capitol Board confronted Superintendent Jasper N. Preston with charges leveled by the two competing archi-

---

[69] Ibid., Mar. 13, 1881. No real hints exist in the articles concerning their authorship except that the writer probably lived in Austin and supposedly had not entered the Capitol competition, but possessed a great deal of knowledge concerning architectural history and current styles. This suggests that either Jacob Larmour or Jasper N. Preston may have written the articles, since neither entered the contest. The fact that Ruffini entered a partnership with Preston in 1877 suggests that Preston wrote the series of articles. The possibility exists also that Ruffini himself wrote them to promote selection of one of his own entries.

[70] Gammel (comp.), *Laws of Texas*, IX, 219 (quotations), 220; *Report of the Capitol Building Commissioners* (1883), 16–17.

[71] *Report of the Capitol Building Commissioners* (1883), 17. Born in Philadelphia, Le Brun studied under Thomas U. Walter, who designed the extension of the United States Capitol in the 1850s. Walter had studied under prominent Philadelphia architect William Strickland, a "disciple of Benjamin H. Latrobe," who exercised much influence on the design of the national Capitol. *Dictionary of American Biography*, s.v. "Le Brun, Napoléon Eugène Henry Charles" (footnote quotation; Withey and Withey, *Biographical Dictionary of American Architects*, 366–367; *The National Cyclopaedia of American Biography* . . . (New York: James T. White & Co., 1891–) IX, 330; Montgomery Schuyler, "The Work of N. Le Brun & Sons," *Architectural Record*, XXVII (May, 1910), 368–381.

tects who lived in Austin, Ruffini and Wahrenberger, that he had accepted money from a contractor in connection with construction of the Williamson County Courthouse in nearby Georgetown. Refusing to respond to the charges, Preston resigned on April 12, nearly two weeks before Le Brun arrived in Austin.[72]

Before and after Le Brun's arrival, rumors abounded. Several newspaper articles indicated erroneously that the commissioners finally had made a decision.[73] On April 23, the day before Le Brun arrived, the Galveston *News* reported that the Capitol Board had met with two of the competing architects and added, "There appears to be some friction in the business, in which the public is supposed to have no interest." The newspaper also noted:

> It was reported in town that the architect to decide between the plans for the State Capitol had arrived, but it was only an exciting canard, occasioned by the arrival of a Brooklyn contractor, who will probably want to make a bid for the contract. It appears to the Capitol Commission that one certain plan of the dozen submitted is so far preferable to all the others that there is no necessity for the auxiliary architect to be imported.[74]

Several days later the paper further reported, "It is rumored that an agent of some of the architects who have submitted plans for the new Capitol is in the city, with corrupt designs and much money, and that Marshal [Ben] Thompson has been detailed to shadow him."[75] In spite of the hiring of Le Brun, the competing architects continued to plead their own cases, as indicated in the Galveston paper on May 1:

> It is evident that there is trouble in store for the State Capitol Commissioners whatever their award may be, as there is great antagonism between the various architects, and the selection of a plan entirely satisfactory is impossible.[76]

After Le Brun had spent several days in Austin, the Galveston paper claimed, "He is disappointed at the lack of that high order of architectural skill in plans submitted that he expected to find, some of the plans, he states, having been submitted in other States as much as five years ago."[77] But finally, in a closed meeting of the Capitol Board on

[72] Minutes [Minute Book], State Capitol Board (May 16, 1879–July 18, 1881), 18–21, Capitol Building Commission Records (Archives Division, Texas State Library, Austin).

[73] Austin *Daily Statesman*, Apr. 1, 26, 1881; San Antonio *Daily Express*, Apr. 22, 1881; Galveston *Daily News*, Apr. 23, 1881.

[74] Galveston *Daily News*, Apr. 23, 1881.

[75] Ibid., Apr. 27, 1881.

[76] Ibid., May 1, 1881.

[77] Ibid., May 5, 1881. Le Brun may have been referring to those previously entered in the Indiana competition by Ruffini and in the Kentucky competition by Andrewartha, as well as others.

May 6, Le Brun recommended "with certain modifications" the plan submitted under the name "Tuebor" by Elijah E. Myers. The next day the board formally accepted Le Brun's recommendation.[78] The inexperience of the Capitol Board and building commissioners with the construction of a large building undoubtedly caused Le Brun to suggest:

> The information your Commissioners would derive by visiting some of the most celebrated State capitol buildings, lately finished or in course of execution, would be of great benefit and interest to the State in carrying out the erection of your projected grand building.[79]

Myers agreed to most of the changes suggested by Le Brun as well as the board's request "to alter the form of the dome" from square to round, similar to the dome on the national Capitol. In addition to the $1,700 prize, the board agreed to pay Myers $12,000 to prepare "working details, covering every minutiae [*sic*] of construction," a bargain fee at the time for a structure estimated to cost $1,500,000. Myers invited the Capitol Board to send someone to Detroit to examine the plans being drawn for the Texas Capitol, as well as to visit the Michigan Capitol at Lansing, which he had designed nine years earlier. In September, 1881, land commissioner William C. Walsh traveled to Detroit and Lansing and "derived much valuable information from the observations made and explanations furnished him."[80]

Newspapers around the state promptly announced the winner and indicated a general satisfaction with the choice. The Galveston *Daily News* claimed, "Everybody seems to be satisfied with the selection except a few competing architects."[81] The same newspaper further commented editorially:

> The active canvass for the designs of some local architects must have exerted a painful pressure upon the commissioners, and it is likely that a corresponding depression in the lobby would follow an unexpected decision in favor of a Michigan architect.[82]

Several days after announcing Le Brun's selection of the winning plan, the Austin *Daily Statesman* commented, "as a matter of justice to our home talent," that Le Brun had regarded one of Ruffini's entries

---

[78] *Report of the Capitol Building Commissioners* (1883), 20.

[79] Ibid.

[80] Ibid., 17–20, 21 (1st and 2nd quotations), 28 (3rd quotation).

[81] Galveston *Daily News*, May 8, 1881; Austin *Daily Statesman*, May 8, 1881; San Antonio *Evening Light*, May 10, 1881; San Antonio *Daily Express*, May 8, 9, 1881.

[82] Galveston *Daily News*, May 8, 1881.

"as *second* best of all the designs submitted."[83] This article, together with the two earlier articles in the Austin paper about Ruffini's design, probably caused local architects Andrewartha and Wahrenberger, who had established a partnership, to take issue with the *Statesman* for encouraging selection of one of the plans. In their letter to the newspaper in late May, 1881, the two architects also criticized the judge of the competition: "Le Brun's questionable standing in the profession, and the crude, unsatisfactory, contradictory and one-sided exparte character of . . . [his report], and his specious arguments to advance the single interest of the plan selected is [*sic*] well known."[84]

Six months later the Austin *Daily Statesman* indicated that Andrewartha planned to sue Myers. According to the paper, in his petition Andrewartha alleged that Myers had hired an agent who wrote a letter containing "libelous matter" concerning Andrewartha's work in Kentucky. Andrewartha further contended that, "to benefit himself and others," Myers had shown the letter to several persons in Austin and also circulated it through Ruffini and Preston. For some reason, however, Andrewartha failed to press suit.[85]

Seven years after Le Brun's selection of the Capitol design by Myers, Texas dedicated its new statehouse with a week of festivities that included fireworks, militia drills, a parade, speeches, and a ball, but nothing indicates that Myers attended the celebration. During the intervening years from 1881 to 1888, the Capitol Board had both requested and agreed to many alterations in the plans drawn by the Detroit architect. In addition, in spite of the care in selecting an architect for the new Capitol, the board effectively fired Myers in early 1886 because he refused to respond to its questions and its frequent demands for him to come inspect work on the new building.[86]

Politics, bitter rivalries among several of the competing architects, the fact that Myers knew of the plan to build a new Capitol as early as

---

[83] Austin *Daily Statesman*, May 21, 1881. A few days after the board approved the design submitted by Myers, Ruffini applied to Governor Roberts for the position of superintendent that had been vacated earlier by Preston, "trusting that the flattering position, (as second) awarded me by the expert, in the late competition for plans for State House, may entitle my claim to some consideration." F. E. Ruffini to Roberts in Governors' Papers: O. M. Roberts.

[84] Austin *Daily Statesman*, May 25, 1881.

[85] Ibid., Nov. 2, 1881.

[86] See the several printed reports of the Capitol Building Commissioners from 1883 to 1888 for details concerning the various changes: *Report of the Capitol Building Commissioners* (1883); *Report of the Capitol Building Commission to the Governor of Texas* . . . (Austin: E. W. Swindells, State Printer, 1885); *Third Biennial Report of the Capitol Building Commission* . . . (Austin: Triplett & Hutchings, State Printers, 1886); *Report of the Capitol Building Commission* . . . (Austin: Hutchings Printing House, 1888); *Final Report of the Capitol Building Commissioners* . . . (Austin: State Printing Office, 1888); *Final Report of the Secretary of State Capitol Board* (Austin: State Printing Office, 1888).

1879, probably through a friendship with Preston, the naivete of Texas officials concerning architecture as well as competitions, and the tenacious frugality that permeated state government, all played important roles in the Texas Capitol competition in 1881. More sophisticated than other newspapers in the state, the Galveston *Daily News* spoke out in vain against parsimonious state officials who wished to obtain the best design but refused to spend the money to do so. Finally, choosing a design for the new Capitol became "a question of great delicacy," causing the Capitol Board to relinquish the opportunity and responsibility of choosing a design for the new statehouse to an expert from the East. Notwithstanding this effort to insure that the selection would be judicious and well informed, some evidence exists that Myers resorted to unethical and even illegal means to win the competition.

Nonetheless, the magnificent red granite structure that resulted from Napoleon Le Brun's decision in May, 1881, reflects great credit on the abilities of Elijah E. Myers, as well as on the determination of the Capitol Board to choose the best plan. Furthermore, none of the competing architects except Myers achieved much prominence beyond their own localities, either before or after the Texas Capitol competition. Besides designing the Michigan and Texas capitols, Myers won competitions in 1885 to design capitols for Colorado and for Idaho Territory. Three years later the Colorado officials also fired Myers, but that same year a building commission in Utah Territory retained him to design a capitol that was never constructed. In addition, Myers reputedly designed a never-built Parliament building for Brazil. Thus, in spite of the various allegations and any chicanery on the part of Myers, Texas obtained plans for an extraordinary statehouse by the only competing architect who ever had designed or ever would design another state capitol.[87]

---

[87] Koellner, "Elijah E. Myers," 46–47, 49–51; Heck, "The Practice of E. E. Myers," 69.

The Designing Architect: Elijah E. Myers

ELIJAH E. MYERS, ARCHITECT OF THE TEXAS CAPITOL, LEFT A LEGACY of impressive public buildings, but as a biographical subject his middle initial might well stand for Enigma. His childhood and youth can be traced to Philadelphia, but there are no reminiscences of family, teachers, or friends.[1] We know of no religious or philosophical creed that directed his actions or sustained him in adversity. His wife and children are shadowy figures—even the son who became his professional partner. Our principal sources of information on the man behind the buildings are the business correspondence and official minutes in the archives of the cities, counties, and states that were his clients in one of the most geographically extensive architectural practices of the late nineteenth century. Although these papers are formal in tone, as suits a contractual relationship, they cannot conceal the strained tempers and frustrations of dealing at a distance with a man whose arrogance and deviousness so frequently betrayed his genius. Much that might have been said was probably withheld as improper or embarrassing.

Myers's career coincides with a period of revolutionary changes in the profession of architecture in the United States. In 1863, when he first advertised himself as an architect in Springfield, Illinois, there was no academic training in any American university to provide professional credentials, and no Americans had yet returned from formal architectural studies in Europe.[2] Apprenticeship was not monitored by a professional guild and in most cases was not thought necessary. At the

---

*Paul Goeldner is chief of the Historic Resource Services Division in the Office of Professional Services in the National Capitol Region of the National Park Service. A registered architect in Texas, Goeldner received his doctorate from Columbia University and served on the architecture faculty at Texas Tech University. He is the author of the *Texas Catalog: Historic American Buildings Survey* (1974) and the *Utah Catalog: Historic American Buildings Survey* (1979).

[1] Martha Ann Kuepper Koellner, "Elijah E. Myers (1832–1909), Architect" (M.A. thesis, Western Illinois University, 1972), 2.

[2] Ibid.

Photograph of Elijah E. Myers, c. 1885. *Courtesy State Preservation Board.*

same time, the unprecedented expansion of the young nation demanded buildings of greater and greater size and quality.

By 1900, when Myers's career was waning, the profession was beginning to be dominated by architects with academic training in American universities. The American Institute of Architects had become a strong national organization after healing regional animosities of the 1880s. Laws to examine and register architects were in effect in several states. Technology had developed better building materials, engineering techniques, and such benefits to office management as the typewriter, the telegraph, and blueprinting.

Although Elijah Myers designed residences and churches, he is best known for the volume of his public work in an era when architects were selected by competition for city halls, courthouses, and state capitols. So much time and money could be invested in an unsuccessful proposal that it is easy to understand Myers's hostility toward other competing architects. While the AIA was working to change the system of selecting architects, Myers attempted to beat the system. Some of his successes survive to demonstrate his talents, but he was not able to keep up the pace he set for himself. Many of his greatest achievements were compromised by ethical and legal questions that he could not completely conceal from potential clients. His attempts to cover his tracks will always frustrate his biographers.[3]

In the 1860 census, Elijah E. Myers and his wife, Mary, ages twenty-eight and twenty-three respectively, were recorded as living in the Frankford section of Philadelphia. He identified himself as a master carpenter. In the 1870 census they were located in Springfield, Illinois, and Myers was listed as an architect. The couple had a six-year-old son, George, and a three-year-old daughter, Julia, both born in Illinois. The only surprise in these records is that Elijah had aged fourteen years while Mary was only seven years older. Such deception is relatively innocent, but it reveals a casual attitude toward the truth that casts doubt on anything else they might say about themselves.

In February, 1870, the Macoupin County Courthouse in Carlinville, Illinois, was completed. An impressive structure by today's standards, it demonstrated Myers's mastery of his profession. Its records show that he also participated in the graft that drove its cost to $1,342,000, a phe-

---

[3] *Tract on Competitions* as presented by the Committee on Professional Practice. Ordered printed by the Ninth Annual Convention, American Institute of Architects, held at the Library Room of the Maryland Historical Society, Baltimore, Wednesday, November 17, 1875.

Official documents do not provide a physical description of Myers, but he must have had a charisma not evident in mere letters and photographs. His physical descriptions of his buildings are amusing to academic architectural taxonomists, but he was an adept designer whose terminology was less outrageous than that of modern real-estate promotions.

nomenal figure for its day. His fees, which included $3,700 for travel expenses, totaled almost $60,000, excluding other income from probable profits on specified building materials. His commission was nearly ten percent of the estimated real value of the building as determined by Charles H. Pond, the St. Louis architect who was hired by the next county administration to help determine the extent to which the taxpayers had been swindled.[4]

With that comfortable nest egg, Myers was prepared to enter the competition to design the state capitol of Michigan. Michigan's Board of State Building Commissioners had received competition entries from sixteen architects, each identified by a pseudonym. Much too bulky to be put in a vault, the drawings were kept in a locked room until those making the selection could meet early in 1872.[5] "Tuebor," the name that identified Myers's entries in both the Michigan and Texas competitions, is from the Michigan coat of arms and means "I will defend." Anonymity in such a competition was probably not achievable. We know that Myers had exchanged correspondence with Governor Henry P. Baldwin in March and April, 1871, in his words, "to ascertain your views in regard to your State House design."[6]

After he was awarded the commission, but before he moved his office and family to Detroit for more convenient supervision, it seems noteworthy that Myers used Judge Thaddeus Loomis as a messenger to send samples of marble to Governor Baldwin. A resident of Carlinville, Loomis had been one of the commissioners on the Macoupin County Courthouse project and had also shared significantly in the graft.[7]

While the Michigan Capitol was under construction (1873–1879), Myers's conduct seems to have been a model of professional behavior. He kept costs close to the budget; the $1,427,743 total was a bargain for buildings of that character. At the dedication, the Michigan House of Representatives expressed gratitude that the capitol "passes into the possession of the state not only free from debt, but absolutely free also from the odor of fraud."[8]

A number of lesser projects kept Myers occupied through the 1870s, including courthouses in Marshall, Michigan, and Danville, Illinois,

[4]County Court Record, Macoupin County, Volume D, 50 (Carlinville, Illinois); *History of Macoupin County* (Philadelphia: Brink, McDonough & Co., 1879), 48.

[5]A. L. Bours to Henry P. Baldwin, Dec. 28, 1871, Executive Office Records, Accession No. 44 (History Division, Michigan State Archives).

[6]Elijah E. Myers to Baldwin, Apr. 24, 1871, ibid.

[7]Myers to Baldwin, Apr. 5, 1872, ibid.; County Court Record, Macoupin County, Volumes C and D include repeated entries in which Judge Loomis and County Clerk George Holliday appropriate money to themselves for "sundry services to the county."

[8]*Journal of the House of the State of Michigan,* I, 44–45.

a state hospital in Pontiac, Michigan, and residences in Marshall and Detroit. None of these took him far from home or involved unusual magnitude or complexity. By November, 1880, when the Capitol Building Commissioners of Texas published a *Notice to Architects* soliciting building plans and specifications, his commissions included courthouse projects in Elyria, Ohio, and Denver, Colorado. The central arch that characterizes the principal facade of the Texas Capitol was also a feature of his Arapahoe County Courthouse in Denver. That building was razed in 1933.[9]

The Texas State Capitol represents the pinnacle of Elijah Myers's career. He would no doubt have agreed—the building is pictured on letterheads that he used as late as 1896. The Capitol displays his abilities at their best, and before it was completed it had exposed him at his worst, as well.

Much can be learned about the practice of public architecture in 1880 by careful consideration of the commissioners' *Notice to Architects*. It is a model document for evaluating the adequacy of competitive submissions, showing that the commissioners, who were new to their role, must have had good professional help. Requirements for lighting, heating, ventilating, acoustics, and fireproofing follow a long list of necessary rooms and their functions. The orientation of the principal facade (south) is specified, as well as the material for the superstructure (stone) and the building's worth ($1,500,000). The statement that "estimates may be based upon the fact that stone, brick, lime and sand can be procured within from one to five miles from the ground" later proved untrue.[10]

Architects competing for a single $1,700 prize were expected to submit drawings that included a foundation plan, first-floor plan, second-floor plan, third-floor plan, roof plan, longitudinal section, transverse section, front elevation, rear elevation, and end elevation. A perspective drawing was optional. Complete specifications were also to be provided. Submissions were to be accompanied by sealed identifications; the right to reject any and all plans was reserved.

Imagine reading such a notice, realizing that one had about three months in which to prepare and submit a design and knowing that only one entrant would be reimbursed for his efforts. The unfairness of uncompensated architectural services was a rallying point in the organization of the American Institute of Architects. However, while other ar-

---

[9] Koellner, "Elijah E. Myers," 20–31. The *Notice to Architects* is reprinted in *Report of the Capitol Building Commissioners to the Governor of Texas, Austin, January 1, 1883* (Austin: E. W. Swindells, State Printer, 1883), 14.

[10] *Report of the Capitol Building Commissioners* (1883), 14.

chitects hesitated to invest their time and talent for a very uncertain reward, Myers confidently accepted the challenge. Competition, by fair means or foul, seems to have been an essential part of his personality, as professional cooperation was not.

There were no shortcuts to winning the Texas Capitol competition. The commissioners not only required anonymity in the submissions, but also devised a sixteen-point scoring system by which the eleven entries could be evaluated evenhandedly. This was further refined "through more than one hundred parallels of comparison, embracing every essential, from foundation to dome." Legislation also authorized the commissioners to engage the services of an expert architect to "assist in the examination and selection of plans."[11]

With this authority and through the offices of Congressman Roger Q. Mills, they brought Napoleon Le Brun from New York to Austin at a cost of $3,000 plus travel expenses. The extent of Myers's work in preparing competition drawings is apparent in the detailed analysis and recommendations for modification that accompanied Le Brun's selection of "the set of plans sent under the *nom de plume* of Tuebor."[12]

May, 1881, was a time of unanimity and good feeling. All of those involved in the selection of an architect were in agreement. When notified of his selection, Myers came promptly to Austin and accepted all the proposed changes, agreeing to make corrected drawings without additional charge.[13]

But in a competition of this type, the number of losers is always proportional to the number of competitors, and at least one, John Andrewartha of Austin, expressed his dissatisfaction with Myers's selection in a published letter objecting that the design was not sufficiently "Southern in its origin and in its arrangements." He later sued Myers for libel and conspiracy to destroy Andrewartha's reputation through false representations to Bradstreet's agency.[14]

---

[11] Ibid., 15, 16 (quotations). In addition to the sources referred to in this article, readers seeking accessible, published information on Myers and the Texas State Capitol should consult the following: Paul Goeldner (comp.), *Texas Catalog: Historic American Buildings Survey*, ed. Lucy Pope Wheeler and S. Allen Chambers, Jr. (San Antonio: Trinity University Press, 1974), 18–20, 61; Roxanne Kuter Williamson, *Austin, Texas: An American Architectural History* (San Antonio: Trinity University Press, 1973), 4, 52–53, 81, 90–95; Willard B. Robinson, *Texas Public Buildings of the Nineteenth Century* (Austin: University of Texas Press for the Amon Carter Museum of Western Art, 1974), 206, 260, 265.

[12] *Report of the Capitol Building Commissioners* (1883), 17 (quotation), 18–20.

[13] Ibid., 21. Records and correspondence between Myers and his Texas Capitol clients refer to him as Colonel E. E. Myers, a rank unearned in military service and one that Myers himself never used, though he did not discourage later clients from adopting the practice. This Texas gesture of approval and honor has had the unhappy effect of sending scholars on fruitless searches of military records to support speculation about his service in the Union Army Corps of Engineers.

[14] Austin *Daily Statesman*, May 25 (quotation), Nov. 2, 1881.

Awarded a $12,000 contract to prepare detailed working drawings and specifications, Myers completed and returned them to Austin by early October to permit the receipt of contractors' sealed bids by November 15.[15] The success of the architect-client relationship at this point was based on a strong community of interest that was not destined to last. After the construction contract was awarded, the Capitol Building Commissioners became involved in a protracted controversy over the selection of building stone, a subject in which Myers was only peripherally involved, amenable to whatever choice was made. With his reputation enhanced by his selection as architect of the Texas State Capitol, Myers overextended his practice to projects and competitions in at least eleven other states, from Virginia to California.

Preparing plans and specifications for a large construction project is similar to outfitting a lengthy sea voyage or safari. The omission or neglect of even a small item can become a crucial, costly problem after the enterprise is under way. If the architect is available to correct unforeseen errors, they can often be minimized. Some Texas clients, like the Dallas County Commissioners Court, hired an architect not only as a designer but as a resident superintendent. During the construction of the Dallas County courthouse in 1891 the architect, M. A. Orlopp, Jr., took a three-day leave to go to Little Rock only after the court had granted permission.[16]

Records make it clear that Myers was the "designing" architect of the Texas Capitol. Though he was not expected to supervise construction, he was expected to resolve disputes regarding design intentions and to come to Austin occasionally to comment on the adequacy of the work at its various stages. For the most part, however, the success of the undertaking was dependent on the completeness, correctness, and availability of the construction drawings.

The commissioners gave high priority to making duplicate plans. Their $300 investment in a set of blueprints failed to meet their needs, not because the Texas sun was too weak to expose the print paper, but because the process required a larger sheet of distortion-free glass than was obtainable and because the process would not reproduce the color designations on the originals.[17] The work necessary to create and reproduce the originals by hand and the commissioners' anxiety to get the job done properly are apparent in a request to Myers to send six to ten draftsmen from Detroit.[18] Eleven days later the commissioners re-

---

[15] *Report of the Capitol Building Commissioners* (1883), 21.

[16] Dallas County Commissioners Court, Minutes, Vol. 4, Nov. 16, 1891, p. 199.

[17] *Report of the Capitol Building Commissioners* (1883), 34.

[18] Joseph Lee and Nimrod L. Norton to Myers, May 16, 1882, Letter Press Book, 1, Capitol Building Commission Records (Archives Division, Texas State Library, Austin).

sponded to his reply, reducing their request to just three. They had hired others locally.[19]

This same letter is probably the first reference to Myers's son George as an assistant in his father's firm. The commissioners agreed that he would be acceptable to accompany the draftsmen and check their work. It is unclear whether the commissioners had been told that George was only eighteen years old.

The duplicate set of drawings was begun on June 3, 1882, and not completed until September 22. The law required the work to be performed in the presence of the commissioners and that each copy be approved by the designing architect. This necessitated continuous attendance of the commissioners in the drafting room and two trips to Austin for architect Myers. The first eighteen plates were approved and sent to the contractor in Chicago in August, and the remaining twenty-one plates, almost seven weeks later.[20]

On Myers's recommendation, the commissioners appointed W. D. Clark of Springfield, Illinois, as superintendent of construction. Since they first contacted him in Denver, it is probable that he had supervised the construction of Myers's Arapahoe County Courthouse, which was nearing completion. He assumed his responsibilities in Texas on November 20.[21]

The records indicate that the Texas Capitol Building Commissioners took their responsibilities very seriously, especially with regard to the selection and approval of concrete and building stone. The weight of political sentiment was insistent that Texas materials be used, particularly where they would be visible. Although the contractor promoted Indiana limestone as superior, physically and economically, to the local limestone that was originally specified, it was both inevitable and justifiable that he would accede to a later decision to use Texas granite for all exterior walls, the stone to be quarried by convict labor.[22]

For the designing architect, the change to a granite building required a simplification of his perspective drawing by eliminating the Corinthian porticoes on each end of the building and changing the recommended textured finish of the stone. Although the discussions and negotiations regarding the change from limestone to granite were so lengthy that they ultimately added two years to the contracted comple-

[19] Jno. T. Dickinson to Myers, May 27, 1882, ibid., 11–12.

[20] *Report of the Capitol Building Commissioners* (1883), 36–37.

[21] Ibid., 39; Oran M. Roberts to W. D. Clark, Oct. 3, 1882, Letter Press Book, 92–93, Capitol Building Commission Records.

[22] Robinson, *Texas Public Buildings*, 260–261.

tion date, Myers was increasingly criticized for his failure to provide prompt responses to questions from the commission and superintendent. With reference to his provision of the revised perspective and specifications, the record says, "After some correspondence with Colonel Myers, he finally furnished the information desired."[23] This was in January, 1885.

Inasmuch as the Texas records show infrequent references to Myers through 1883 and 1884, it is appropriate to follow other projects in which he was involved. On October 25, 1882, two years after the original acceptance of Myers's design, the cornerstone of the Douglas County Courthouse in Omaha was laid. At some time earlier in the year work had begun on the Harper Hospital in Detroit, after Myers had deleted two wings to bring the project within the budget.[24]

An awkward situation for Myers occurred on November 11, 1882, when only two of the commissioners of Seneca County, Ohio, met to "appoint, select and employ" him as architect for a new courthouse. Five days later the commission voted to give further consideration to plans of other architects, but on December 26 it reversed itself again, rescinded the resolution revoking Myers's employment, and invited him to come to Tiffin to arrange a contract. The next ten months were spent in raising the appropriation and lowering the bids so that a contract could be awarded on September 22, 1883.[25]

Myers so frequently insisted that his designs could be constructed within his estimates and the available appropriation, when they so rarely could, that he might well be accused of incompetence or dishonesty. Another possibility is that he so desperately wanted his designs to be built that he believed, and convinced others to believe, that his estimates were sound. Since he also had a reputation for fee cutting, the extra work necessary to bring down initial costs would have reduced his income painfully unless he was able to recoup his losses through later fees and kickbacks.

In September, 1883, Myers, who must have been feeling very confident about his reputation, sought the most prestigious architectural post in the federal government, that of supervising architect of the Treasury Department. From that office came the designs for post offices, customhouses, federal courthouses, and other buildings that rep-

---

[23] *Third Biennial Report of the Capitol Building Commission . . . to the Governor of Texas, Austin, November 1, 1886* (Austin: Triplett & Hutchings, State Printers, 1886), 8.

[24] Koellner, "Elijah E. Myers," 35, 36.

[25] Commissioners Journal, Seneca County, Tiffin, Ohio, Vol. 7, pp. 179 (quotation), 184, 200, 424–430.

resented the national government in major cities and ports. Among the recommendations submitted on Myers's behalf was one from the Capitol Building Commissioners of Texas, who took "pleasure in recommending him as an Architect preeminent in his profession," whose plans for the Texas State Capitol had been pronounced "the most minute, complete, and elaborate ever prepared for any public building in America."[26]

At the same time he was one of five architects invited to submit designs for the Allegheny County Courthouse and Jail in Pittsburgh. The winner of that competition, Henry H. Richardson, has been so honored by later architectural historians and critics that it is hard to believe he was the last of the competitors to be invited. His death in April, 1886, before the project was completed in 1888, encouraged a wave of imitative architecture by admirers who might have hesitated to mimic a living master. Myers's most Richardsonian work is the Central Methodist Episcopal Church in Lansing, which was begun in 1888.[27]

When Mifflin E. Bell received the appointment as supervising architect of the Treasury Department, Myers wrote to the secretary of the treasury in October, 1883: "Sir, Please return to me by Express C.O.D. the papers and recommendations filed with my application for appointment as Supervising Architect. They are valuable as expressions of friendship and as they are no further use to you, it would gratify me to have and preserve them."[28]

In November, 1883, Myers submitted plans for a city hall for Richmond, Virginia, which eventually were used. In January, 1884, his design for the Allegheny County buildings was displayed in Pittsburgh with those of the three other competitors who had submitted complete projects. Richardson's success was announced in February.[29]

Myers visited Austin on January 18, 1884.[30] He could report that the concrete work for the foundations of the Capitol was done entirely to his satisfaction. But his visit was poorly timed. He claimed, as he would

---

[26] Lee and Norton to Charles J. Folger, Sept. 14, 1883, Letter Press Book, 280 (quotations), 281, Capitol Building Commission Records.

[27] James D. Van Trump, Editor, *Charette: Pennsylvania Journal of Architecture*, to P. G., May 8, 1969; Koellner, "Elijah E. Myers," 55–56. Significant differences between Richardson and Myers are as obvious in their personalities as in their architecture. Richardson gave tremendous stature to his profession in America and internationally by the quantity and quality of his friendships.

[28] Myers to Folger, Oct. 30, 1883, General Records of the Department of the Treasury, Record Group 56 (National Archives).

[29] Van Trump to P. G., May 8, 1969; Mariana Griswold Van Rensselaer, *Henry Hobson Richardson and His Works* (New York: Houghton, Mifflin & Co., 1888), 89.

[30] *Report of the Capitol Building Commission to the Governor of Texas, Austin, January 1, 1885* (Austin: E. W. Swindells, State Printer, 1885), 18.

on many future occasions, that he had been detained by illness. Because the commissioners were involved in a session of the legislature, he was too late to meet with them and too early to confer with General R. Lindsay Walker, who did not assume his responsibilities as superintendent of construction until February 11.

Called away on other business, he resolved none of the issues raised in a lengthy letter conveying Governor John Ireland's displeasure with accusatory and evasive responses to questions addressed to Myers in December. He also was asked in that letter to explain his demand for the resignation of W. D. Clark as superintendent of construction.[31]

Illness might explain Myers's sending his twenty-year-old son George to represent him before the Richmond City Council, which was considering the merits of enlarging the appropriation to enable the construction of Myers's design. As his father might have done, George assured the council that granite could be substituted for brick and a heating plant included without altering the $300,000 cost.[32] Bids were received in both August and December, 1884, and at neither time could a builder be found to work within the limit as promised by the architect.

Elijah Myers's most positive accomplishment of 1884 was the preparation of drawings for the Knox County Courthouse in Galesburg, Illinois. His contract with the county paid him $4,000 and guaranteed a building that could be erected for $100,000, exclusive of the steam heating system. Though it was an otherwise tempestuous period in his career, Myers remained on the best of terms with Knox County throughout the project and was honored at the dedication on January 26, 1888, even though the final cost exceeded $146,000.[33]

Although his correspondence with Texas indicated that he spent most of the year sick in bed, 1885 was possibly the busiest year in Myers's career. In the spring he prepared a winning design for the Idaho Territorial Capitol, on which construction was begun in June. In March he again made himself available for the post of supervising architect of the Treasury Department, soliciting recommendations from the architect brother-in-law of the newly inaugurated Grover Cleveland and from a Detroit lawyer who identified himself as a "somewhat prominent" Democrat in Michigan.[34] President Cleveland chose

---

[31] Dickinson to Myers, Dec. 4, 1883, Letter Press Book, 337–340, Capitol Building Commission Records.

[32] Louise Heite, "A Document in Stone, City Hall, Richmond, Virginia, 1886–1894," unpublished ms., Jan. 1970, p. 4.

[33] Board of Supervisors Record, New Court House, Knox County, 11–15, 248.

[34] Koellner, "Elijah E. Myers," 46; N. B. Bacon to D. S. Lamont, Mar. 11, 1885, RG 56; John Cummings to William C. Whitney, Mar. 12, 1885, ibid.; James Woodruff Romeyn to Daniel Manning, Mar. 12, 1885 (quotation), ibid.

to keep M. E. Bell on the job for another two years, without regard to party affiliation.

On March 12 Myers and six other achitects were invited to come to Hamilton, Ohio, on March 27 to present floor plans and elevations for a fireproof courthouse for Butler County. Myers again was in competition with H. H. Richardson, who in this case was the only architect not representing himself in person. A motion to invite and pay Myers, Richardson, and D. W. Gibbs of Toledo to return with more complete plans failed, and Gibbs was selected.[35]

On April 16 the state of Colorado published a *Notice to Architects* soliciting competitive designs for the Capitol building, with a July 10 deadline. The announcement impelled Myers to activity. On May 5 he wrote to John L. Routt, a member of the Board of Capitol Managers, requesting an extended deadline, pointing out that six months was allowed for the Michigan Capitol and five for the Cincinnati Board of Trade, a current competition awarded to H. H. Richardson that August. On May 21, on the letterhead of "George W. Myers, Architect and Superintendent, Modern Residences and Storefronts Specialties," he wrote to George T. Clark, clerk of the board, offering to pay Clark's expenses to Omaha, where the Douglas County Courthouse would be dedicated on May 28. The meeting would enable Myers to ask a great many questions "regarding the arrangements of the Capitol" and show Clark a "very elegant building." Myers indicated that he could not spare time in his preparation of plans for the Colorado Capitol to travel all the way to Denver.[36]

At that moment, nothing could have been more unwelcome at Myers's Detroit office than the June 6 resolution of the Texas Capitol Board summoning him to Austin on or before July 1, at his own expense, to correct mistakes in his plans. Otherwise the attorney general was authorized to institute a suit for breach of contract. Faced with a choice of honoring a past commitment that he was finding troublesome, or devoting his full attention to an appealing opportunity, he waited for two weeks; on June 22 his son wrote that his father "was so ill that no matters of business could be presented to him."[37] Although the resolution of June 6 was referred to the Texas attorney general on July 9, it was not immediately dealt with.

---

[35] Minutes, Building Committee for New Courthouse, 1885, Butler County, Ohio, 2, 4.

[36] Myers to John L. Routt, May 5, 1885, Department of Administration, State Buildings Plans (Colorado State Archives); Myers to George T. Clark, May 21, 1885, ibid. This collection is cited hereafter as DA, SBP.

[37] *Third Biennial Report*, 28, 34 (quotation).

Of the twenty-one sets of plans submitted for the Colorado State Capitol competition, five were selected for further consideration. At the top of the list was that of Myers, identified as "Corinthian" but of dubious anonymity. The five architects submitting the favored plans were required to prepare detailed estimates supporting the claim that they could be constructed for under $1 million. Myers's estimate, totaling $959,615, was sent from Detroit on July 20.[38]

On August 16 Myers attempted to repair his relations with the Texas Capitol Building Commissioners with a letter agreeing to contract changes published on July 25 and offering to come to Austin any time after October 1. He added, "I have been quite ill most of the summer, and will not be able to come to Texas before that time."[39]

Only two days before, in a letter to Colorado, he referred not to his poor health but to the miserable weather in Detroit and the further gloom of mourning over the death of President Ulysses S. Grant. His selection as designing architect of the Colorado Capitol threw him into another big effort to complete the detailed working drawings, which he began after a trip to Denver in late August to meet with the Board of Capitol Managers.[40]

After an exchange of letters and telegrams, Myers "finally" reached Austin on October 8 to inspect the progress of work on the Capitol and to respond to many questions from the commissioners. Not surprisingly, he answered only some of the questions before "urgently pressing professional engagements" required his presence elsewhere.[41]

If Colorado and Texas had compared notes, they would have found his next claims to illness to be in agreement. On October 30 he wrote to Denver, "After three weeks being confined to my bed with fever, I am again at my office." On November 3 he wrote to Austin, "since my return from Austin, I have been confined to my house with bilious fever, and only able to come to my office on Saturday last." Each letter continued with responsive professional information, and the Texans received a promise to come in January.[42]

Understandably, Myers's time was spent almost entirely on the Colorado project; he wrote to the secretary of the Colorado Capitol Board on November 29 and December 12 describing the extent of his labors

---

[38] Board of Capitol Managers, Minute Book A (Colorado State Archives); Myers to Clark, July 20, 1885, DA, SBP.

[39] *Third Biennial Report*, 43.

[40] Myers to Clark, Aug. 14, 1885, DA, SBP; Board of Capitol Managers, Minute Book A, 68.

[41] *Third Biennial Report*, 43 (1st quotation), 44 (2nd quotation).

[42] Myers to Clark, Oct. 30, 1885, DA, SBP; *Third Biennial Report*, 45–46 (2nd quotation).

and his plans to bring the completed drawings to Denver for a meeting of the board on December 26. On the day he was to leave Detroit, December 23, he wrote to the Texas commissioners giving reasons for not meeting their deadline for modified roof construction plans. Their response of December 29 described this letter as "not at all satisfactory." They insisted that he "come at once" or be replaced. Son George, who seems to have been responsible for excuses, telegraphed on January 2 that his father was absent from Detroit and would not return until January 14.[43]

The patience of the commissioners was exhausted; on January 25, 1886, they resolved:

> Whereas, The plans and specifications of the new State capitol have proven defective and insufficient in many respects; and
> Whereas, The Capitol Board has, after repeated efforts, been unable to get Mr. E. E. Myers, the designing architect, to furnish additional or amended plans and specifications, and he has persistently evaded the direct questions asked him by the Board; therefore
> *Resolved,* That the Attorney General be directed to place the bond of said Myers in suit at once.[44]

Myers responded with an extremely lengthy letter to Governor Ireland, in which he attempted to defend his reputation by blaming others for misrepresentation. That elicited an even longer reply from the commissioners.[45] The relationship was severed, not by formal action of the attorney general but by a mutual informal agreement that E. E. Myers and the Texas Capitol project no longer needed each other.

Specific charges made by the commissioners deserve to be quoted because they show more insight into Myers's character than anything else we might find:

> As a designing architect we regard Mr. Myers with admiration, but we emphatically disapprove his mode of transacting business in his attempts to let contracts for various portions of the construction and finishing of buildings of which he is the designing architect; and we fully understand him, when, realizing as he does, from his experience of the past few years, that this capitol building has but little, if any, additional compensation in it for him as designing architect on the part of the State; that he is liable on a contract between himself and the State for the accuracy of his plans, and that at the time of the execution of said contract he entered into it most willingly in his zealous efforts to

---

[43] Myers to Clark, Nov. 29, Dec. 12, 1885, DA, SBP; *Third Biennial Report*, 49, 50 (quotations), 51.

[44] *Third Biennial Report*, 54.

[45] Ibid., 55–67.

secure the final successful adoption of said plans; he now finds this contract, with bond attached, onerous and irksome, and in endeavoring to relieve himself, if possible, from the obligations of this contract, he would adopt any alternative, even though it were the most scurrilous, as indicated by some of the insinuations in his letter, if he thought by so doing it would extricate him from his responsibilities.[46]

From the letter herewith submitted from the Belgium Glass Company to Sub-Contractor Wilke, it will be observed that said company proposes to contract for furnishing all the glass for the building, and notified Mr. Wilke that they had given the designing architect figures for same amounting to $62,000; while Mr. Myers, in a letter to General Walker, which is herewith submitted, offers to furnish this glass to Mr. Wilke, it being required by the specifications to be Belgium Glass, for $88,000.[47]

Mr. Myers himself acknowledges that it is unreasonable to expect him to come to Austin on short notice, as he has important work all over the Union . . . Mr. Myers is to-day engaged in doing for the State of Colorado what he did for the State of Texas several years ago, when, for many weeks and months, he designed and prepared the perspective and original plans and specifications of our capitol building. . . . In course of actual construction, defects in the plans are discovered frequently, and we know of no authority under the contract by which we can stop any portion of the work which is being done according to plans and specifications, when we are thoroughly satisfied that the said construction is neither safe nor proper, and to have the contractor wait until the necessary change is embodied in a memorandum of agreement and forwarded to Detroit, Michigan, for approval or rejection, with the probabilities of being informed, as we have been frequently before, that Mr. Myers is in some remote part of the country and will not return to Detroit for several weeks.[48]

The matter of the glass is particularly significant because it gives us a clue about how Myers supported himself when he was notorious among other architects for cutting his fees to the minimum. The other comments show an evenhanded willingness to give Myers credit where credit was due. They also describe a modus operandi that was ultimately self-destructive.

There were still successes ahead for Myers, who in 1886 at age fifty-four should have been at the peak of his career, but an increasing number of his projects turned sour. After wooing the secretary of the Wyoming Capitol Building Commission in March and April, he was dismayed when the award went to the "Toledo party," D. W. Gibbs. He

---

[46] Ibid., 61.
[47] Ibid.
[48] Ibid., 65–66.

sent two angry follow-up letters after his first request for the return of his competition drawings and other photographs and documents.[49]

A bright spot of 1886 was the acceptance of his design for the San Joaquin County Courthouse in California in October.[50] This was also the year when his firm became E. E. Myers and Son. A circular prepared for the firm contains the advice, "Require your architect *to guarantee his work to be correct.*"

Perhaps the most profound effect that 1886 would have on Myers's career was his changed relationship with W. D. Richardson, a contractor from Springfield, Illinois, with whom he had been associated on several projects. In January he had recommended Richardson in glowing terms to the Colorado board, describing the completeness of his bids for the Grand Rapids City Hall and his qualifications as an engineer. With a touch of humor, he continued, "The only objection I have to him is that he can read plans keenly, and often catches me, and never gives me any quarter before any board, and will come direct at me when I least anticipate it, but I admire him for that, for he stands up for his rights."[51]

Richardson had hardly begun his contract with the state of Colorado when, on April 12, Myers wrote that Richardson was very sick in Grand Rapids. This was followed by several bulletins on the state of Richardson's serious illness. The tone of Myers's correspondence had changed by June, when he realized that Richardson's illness was preventing his posting his bond and was holding up payments to the architect. Two telegrams were followed by a letter in early July to Governor Benjamin Eaton, pleading that no further delay be tolerated.[52]

Before the end of July Myers was made ill by the delay, as is eloquently stated in his son's telegram: "FATHER CONTINUES QUITE ILL CAN YOU LET HIM HAVE SIX THOUSAND TILL RICHARDSON FILES BOND ANSWER." Both Richardson and Myers recovered, but their relationship did not. Myers continued to provide details of the dome and descriptions of the sculptural ornament through 1888, but, as in Texas, the Coloradans decided they did not need him any longer; by the time the cornerstone was laid in 1890 he had been fired. Richardson's criticism may have played a part.[53]

---

[49] Myers to C. N. Potter, May 19 (quotation), 31, June 8, 1886, Capitol Building Commission Correspondence, Record Group 0103, Mar., 1886–Mar., 1888 (Wyoming State Archives and Historical Department).

[50] Koellner, "Elijah E. Myers," 53.

[51] Myers to Clark, Jan. 29, 1886, DA, SBP.

[52] Myers to Clark, Apr. 12, June 7, 1886, ibid.; Myers to Benjamin H. Eaton, July 5, 1886, ibid.

[53] George W. Myers to Dennis Sullivan, July 30, 1886, telegram, ibid.; E. E. Myers to Clark,

On April 5, 1887, the cornerstone was laid for the Richmond City Hall, which may be considered Elijah Myers's last major work. The project was delayed because Myers's design was originally thought too expensive; a rival firm had to be paid $3,100 when its previously adopted plan was rejected. An investigation while the building was under construction considered evidence that Myers had paid a $1,500 bribe to get his plan adopted. When the structure was finally completed in 1894, the $300,000 limit had been stretched to $1.3 million, which was hardly a testimonial for Myers and Son as cost estimators.[54]

Myers could not avoid publicity that was damaging to his reputation. Between 1887 and 1895 his plans for courthouses in at least twelve counties in seven states were unsuccessful in competition. A design for a Utah Territorial Capitol was accepted but never built.[55]

A capsule biography in 1893, probably approved if not written by him, said, "Mr. Myers [*sic*] success has been phenomenal, and is, in fact, due to his close application to detail, he being a practical mechanic and experienced builder, which enables him at all times to guarantee perfect accuracy in carrying out all plans and specifications with which he is entrusted." By that date Myers's career was definitely declining, and he was involved in a series of lawsuits attempting to recover real or imagined damages from Colorado and other projects. It is reported that his death in 1909 was brought on by bad news regarding such a case.[56]

Several important buildings of Myers's design have survived to prove his ability as an architect. They include state capitols in Michigan, Texas, and Colorado; courthouses in Macomb, Carlinville, and Galesburg, Illinois; the Richmond City Hall; and the Central Methodist Episcopal Church in Lansing. Their architect was a talented, dishonest, hard-working, spiteful, clever, unbalanced, self-assured, self-destructive hypochondriac whose story must be pieced together from fragments. He will always be somewhat mysterious, evasive, and much more interesting than many of his more conventional contemporaries.

Aug. 23, Sept. 24, 1888, ibid.; "Description of Statuary," n.d., ibid.; Board of Capitol Managers, Minute Book B, 70–72, ibid.

[54] Heite, "A Document in Stone," 5, 6.

[55] Paul Goeldner, "Temples of Justice: Nineteenth Century County Courthouses in the Midwest and Texas" (Ph.D. diss., Columbia University, 1970), 487; Koellner, "Elijah E. Myers," 57.

[56] *Detroit of Today* (1893), 78 (quotation); Koellner, "Elijah E. Myers," 7.

THE NEW CAPITOL OF TEXAS

Austin printer Charles N. McLaughlin published this lithograph in 1885, while the Capitol was still under construction. Lithographed by Charles Sinz and W. P. Morgan of Cleveland, Ohio, and based on a perspective drawing by architect Elijah E. Myers, it served to satisfy some of the public's curiosity about the new building going up on the hill at the end of Congress Avenue. *Courtesy Prints and Photographs Collection, Center for American History, University of Texas at Austin.*

Emigrant Strikebreakers:
Scottish Granite Cutters and the Texas Capitol Boycott

MARJORY HARPER*

IN THE NINETEENTH CENTURY NORTHEAST SCOTLAND, AND THE CITY OF Aberdeen in particular, came to enjoy an international reputation in the granite industry. This owed much to a flourishing export trade with the United States, particularly in tombstones and similar memorials. But Aberdeen did not export only its dressed and polished stone; many of the quarrymen and especially the masons responsible for these products also found their way to the U.S.A. The majority congregated in the easily accessible New England states, but some went further afield, to the Midwest, California, and Texas. Scots immigrants, settling singly or in small groups, had played an important part in the early history of Texas, but the best-known—and most notorious—influx occurred in 1886, when a large contingent of masons was brought out to cut stone for the new Texas State Capitol in Austin.[1]

Once the United States began to develop its own granite industry after the Civil War, it became interested in purchasing the well-known skills of quarrymen and masons from Scotland. American labor at this time was inadequate and expensive, and Scottish masons in particular were offered good wages to come over and train a native labor force. Although immigrants were also brought in from Cornwall, Devon, and Wales, the majority of the British workmen were Scots, probably mostly from Aberdeen, and it was by no means unusual for around two hun-

*Marjory Harper has a Ph.D. from the University of Aberdeen in Scotland where she is employed as a lecturer in history. Her main publications are two books on emigration, entitled *Emigration from NorthEast Scotland*, volume I, *Willing Exiles*, and volume II, *Beyond the Broad Atlantic* (1988). Her current research interests include interwar emigration from Scotland (1919–1939), the social welfare work of the Countess of Aberdeen, and computer-based research into the backgrounds, university experiences, and subsequent careers of students at Aberdeen University in the nineteenth century.

[1] The Austin *Daily Statesman* of Oct. 2, 1875, mentioned some Scottish stonecutters who had come from St. Louis to work on the new "Cook building" in downtown Austin, and the same newspaper on Mar. 23, 1880, referred to Scottish carpenters employed in Belton, Texas, fifty miles north of Austin. For other references to Scottish settlers in Texas, see Aberdeen *Journal*, Aug. 15, 1866, Nov. 19, 1879; Austin *American-Statesman*, Jan. 24, 1986.

dred granite tradesmen to be lured away from the city each spring to the American quarries and stoneyards.[2] Some settled down permanently, perhaps establishing their own businesses after a time, while others preferred to invest the money they earned in the subsequent opening of a yard back in Aberdeen. But many continued to commute annually across the Atlantic, returning home temporarily in the winter, then re-emigrating in spring at the opening of each succeeding season.

Although the American employers wanted to exploit the Scots' skills in order to develop their own native granite industry, the arrival of these foreign tradesmen was not universally welcomed. Edmund Stevenson, one of the emigrant commissioners at New York, criticized the parasitic attitude of many transient immigrants when he wrote in 1890 that

hundreds and thousands of skilled mechanics—stone-cutters, stone-masons, glass-blowers, locomotive engineers—come regularly to this country every spring, year after year, and stay here until about November. They pay no taxes for our schools, they perform no jury duty, nor are they liable to; they do not perform any of the duties of citizenship, except the protection they get from the city or the state wherever they reside. During all the working season, they are sending their money back home to their wives, their children, and their parents, and at the end of the working season they pack their grip sacks and go back to Europe, spend the winter, and the next year come back here again, and repeat the same thing over and over again. They come into direct competition with American labour; they drive out American labour by their coming here, skilled workmen that they are, and they generally work under the price of American labour. But they earn much more money here, and they can afford to go back there and live for a few months until the working season, and then come back here.[3]

The way in which employers used immigrants to repress wages, break strikes, and destroy attempts at union organization was most bitterly resented by many branches of American labor. In 1885 the growing hostility took legislative form when Congress, largely at the instigation of the Knights of Labor, passed the Alien Contract Labor Law. This act was designed to prevent the introduction into the U.S.A. of foreign contract workers to perform work that was the prerogative of native labor. As a result it became

---

[2] See, for instance, [Aberdeen] *Granite Cutters' Journal*, I–IX (1901–1910) (Aberdeen University Library, Dept. of Manuscripts and Archives, MSS 2655/2/1/1–9; cited hereafter as Aberdeen *GCJ*); Aberdeen *Daily Free Press*, Aberdeen *Evening Express*, Aberdeen *Evening Gazette*, Aberdeen *Journal* (various dates, 1880–1914); House Misc. Doc. No. 572, 50th Cong., 1st Sess., 1888 (serial 2579), 149: evidence of David Dawson (recorded as "Dorson").

[3] W. H. Wilkins, "Immigration troubles of the United States," *Nineteenth Century*, XXX (Oct., 1891), 588.

unlawful for any person, company, partnership or corporation, in any manner whatsoever to prepay the transportation or in any way assist or encourage the importation or migration of any alien or aliens, and any foreigner or foreigners into the United States, its Territories, or the District of Columbia, under contract or agreement . . . made previous to the importation of such [people] to perform labour or service of any kind in the United States.[4]

Guilty parties were to be liable to a fine of $1,000 in respect of each immigrant illegally introduced, while ships' captains who knowingly transported them were to be fined $500 per immigrant and were also to bear the expense of returning them to their place of origin. In practice, however, the act was easily evaded and failed to eradicate the problems that it was meant to solve[5]: since most immigrants did not enter the U.S.A. as contract laborers and did not therefore fall within the remit of the act, the use of aliens to break strikes and keep wages down continued almost unabated.[6]

Until 1906 the American Granite Cutters' Union repeatedly rebuffed suggestions from its Aberdeen counterpart that it should agree to the interchangeability of union cards and benefits. These proposals were rejected on the grounds that since the emigrant traffic was one-sided, the concessions would benefit only the Scots. There was opposition to any proposal to exchange cards with a union whose entry fees were much lower than those of its American counterpart, and criticism of

---

[4]"An Act to prohibit the importation and migration of foreigners and aliens under contract or agreement to perform labour in the United States, its territories and the District of Columbia," United States Statutes at Large, 48th Cong., 1883–1885, vol. XXIII, p. 332, in [American] *Granite Cutters' National Journal*, X (May, 1886), 3 (quotation), cited hereafter as American *GCNJ*.

[5]Failure to define the precise categories to be excluded caused confusion in interpreting the act, successive court interpretations, and many loopholes. For instance, employers could have contract workers shipped to the U.S.A. as cabin passengers, since only steerage passengers were inspected under the law; or they could persuade members of their existing labor force to write home encouraging "friends and relatives" (who were exempt from the law) to come out on the assurance of work. Contract laborers could also be trained in advance to answer official questions in a way that would avoid detection at the port of arrival. See Charlotte Erickson, *American Industry and the European Immigrant, 1860–1885* (Cambridge, Mass.: Harvard University Press, 1957), 170–171, 172 (quotation).

[6]The act had been urged on the government primarily by a small union of skilled craftsmen within the Knights of Labor, the window-glass workers, whose position was threatened by the introduction of contract workers from Europe. They harnessed to their campaign the growing resentment of the American labor movement in general against the misuse of imported labor, by suggesting—erroneously—that immigrant strikebreakers were generally brought in under contract. In this way the wider labor movement (which had not formulated precise proposals for dealing with its problems) was persuaded to support legislation that was much too narrow to meet its needs. The Contract Labor Law applied only to a small minority of highly skilled immigrants who were brought in to perform specific jobs, and failed to restrict the importation of undesirable immigrants to break strikes and lower wages. For further details on the act and its limitations, see Erickson, *American Industry and the European Immigrant*, especially chapters 9 and 10.

those emigrants who did not become citizens of the U.S.A., but who continued to send home the bulk of their earnings.[7]

On the whole, though, as far as the granite trade was concerned, emigrants from northeast Scotland seem to have worked fairly harmoniously alongside their American counterparts. A number of Aberdeen emigrants played an active part in the American Granite Cutters' Union, and opportunities for Scottish granite tradesmen in the U.S.A. were periodically publicized in the union's journal. It also regularly issued warnings against going to places where work was scarce or where there were industrial disputes, and immigrants were sometimes asked not to flood the American labor market too early in the season, before satisfactory agreements had been made between the employers and the union.[8] Prospective emigrants were warned not to believe the false promises of agents who were sent to Aberdeen to recruit labor for strike-bound American quarries and yards. For much of 1887, for instance, the American *Granite Cutters' National Journal* warned tradesmen to keep away from Boston, where union members had been locked out by their employers. When it became known that the employers had advertised in Aberdeen for men, offering inducements that, according to the union, they did not intend to fulfil, the American union made sure that notices appeared in the Aberdeen press reiterating the plea that granite workers should avoid Boston.[9] In 1892 the Aberdeen *Journal* published the contents of a telegram from the secretary of the American Granite Cutters' Union to his opposite number in Aberdeen, again warning Aberdonian tradesmen to keep away from the U.S.A. until a current lockout in the granite trade had ended.[10] Similarly in 1904 the secretary of the union branch in Montreal asked assistance of his Aberdeen counterpart in preventing further local emigration to that city, after two Aberdeen men had arrived "not knowing the exact condition of affairs," and unaware that they had been recruited as strikebreakers.[11]

---

[7] American *GCNJ*, XIII (June, 1890), 1, and ibid., XIV (Nov., 1891), 5. It was felt that if the Scots were thus favored, many unwanted immigrants of other nationalities might masquerade as Scots in order to gain cheap entry to the American granite workers' union. In 1906, however, it was agreed that foreign granite workers coming into the U.S.A. who could present paid-up cards from their home unions would be admitted to the American union on payment of $10. Those with no such card had to pay an initiation fee of $25. Aberdeen *GCJ*, V (Feb., 1906), 2.

[8] See, for instance, Aberdeen *GCJ*, II (Feb., 1903), 11.

[9] American *GCNJ*, XI (July, 1887), 1, 3, 4.

[10] Aberdeen *Journal*, May 9, 1892. See also ibid., May 17, Sept. 29, 1892.

[11] Aberdeen *GCJ*, IV (June, 1904), 6. "We would wish you to inform all Granitecutters within your jurisdiction of the trouble that exists here, and stop them from coming this way, so as to give us a chance to win our cause, which we vouch for is a just one" (ibid.).

But although there is clear evidence of cooperation between granite workers' unions on either side of the Atlantic, on occasions the American warnings were not heeded, and the Aberdeen recruits then came into bitter conflict with the American trade unionists. Perhaps the most acrimonious incident was one that occurred in 1886 and had its origin not in one of the eastern granite centers in which the Aberdeen immigrants most commonly congregated, but in Texas. Since the incident provided the first real test of the Alien Contract Labor Act, it also attracted national attention in the United States.

In November 1875 the Texas legislature decided that a new State Capitol should be erected in Austin, through the appropriation of a large tract of public land. Since Texas, still recovering from the Civil War, had no funds to finance the project, it was specified that the building contract would be paid off solely in land, the state's one major asset. No further action was taken until February 1879, when 3,050,000 acres in the Texas Panhandle were set apart and a Capitol Board was appointed to administer the project.[12] In April 1879 an act to provide for building the Capitol was passed, and in November 1880 (after the land had been surveyed and valued at fifty cents per acre) the Capitol Board appointed a building superintendent and two building commissioners. Out of eleven sets of plans and specifications submitted to the commissioners by February 1881, the design of E. E. Myers of Detroit was accepted, and in July 1881 the commissioners advertised for tenders for construction, specifying that the entire payment would be made in land. The project assumed greater urgency when the old Capitol burned down on November 9, but only two bids were submitted, and on January 1, 1882, the contract for the new State Capitol was awarded to Mattheas Schnell of Rock Island, Illinois. Within twelve days he had assigned three-quarters of his interest in the project to Taylor, Babcock and Company of Chicago, and by the summer he had relinquished his entire interest to this same company.[13]

---

[12] Consisting of the state's governor, comptroller, attorney general, treasurer, and land commissioner. Fifty thousand acres of the land grant were to be sold to pay for the survey. Much of the following information about the early stages in the construction of the new Capitol has been drawn from Frederick W. Rathjen, "The Texas State House: A Study of the Building of the Texas Capitol Based on the Reports of the Capitol Building Commissioners," in *Southwestern Historical Quarterly*, LX (Apr., 1957), 433–462.

[13] J. Evetts Haley, *The XIT Ranch of Texas and the Early Days of the Llano Estacado* (Norman: University of Oklahoma Press, 1967), chap. IV, "The State Capitol and its builders," 49–57. See also Forrest Crissey, "The Vanishing Range," *The Country Gentleman*, LXXVIII, Mar. 1, 1913. Also included in the Chicago syndicate that took over responsibility for constructing the Capitol were United States Senator Charles B. Farwell of Illinois and his younger brother John Farwell. Col. Abner Taylor was the Representative to Congress from Illinois, and his father-in-law Amos Babcock, a large landholder in Illinois, made up the fourth member of the syndicate. Their original intention was to dispose of the Panhandle grant in some speculative scheme. It was only after their failure to sell the land that they decided to operate it as a ranch until increased immigration would raise its value and enable them to sell at a profit. The XIT Ranch

The construction of a new Texas State Capitol was given greater urgency when the existing Capitol was destroyed by fire in November 1881. *Courtesy Austin History Center, Austin Public Library.*

Excavations began in February 1882 and preparation of the foundation and basement occupied that year and most of 1883.[14] It was intended that the superstructure should be built primarily of limestone, and by February 1884 about $100,000 had been spent in quarrying and dressing limestone boulders at the Oatmanville quarry near Austin. In March the railway for transporting the stone from the quarry to the building site was completed, and the first consignment—about sixty tons of limestone—was delivered, only to be rejected by the building commissioners on the grounds that it did not meet the required standard.[15] It subsequently became clear that Texas quarries alone could

---

was accordingly launched with the aid of $15 million raised through the London-based Capitol Freehold Land and Investment Company. For further details, see the Austin *Daily Statesman*, Mar. 4, 1959; and "The Texas Capitol. How it was built," *The Cattleman*, XLVI (Mar., 1960), 42–43, 68–70.

[14] A temporary Capitol was constructed simultaneously. It was to be completed by January 1883 at a cost of no more than $45,000, but both these targets were lost when the half-built structure collapsed on September 7, 1882. Rathjen, "The Texas State House," 439.

[15] The Oatmanville stone contained too much iron pyrites, and exposure to the weather caused it to become discolored, with rusty-colored streaks. Rathjen, "The Texas State House," 442.

not supply enough limestone of the standard specified and contractor Abner Taylor suggested that limestone from Bedford, Indiana, be substituted for the Oatmanville product. This, however, would have required a major change in the terms of the contract and would go against the state's policy of using only Texas products. Reserves of red Texas granite near Burnet were then beginning to attract notice, and state governor John Ireland (who headed the Capitol Board) was strongly supported by public opinion when he recommended changing the specifications for the Capitol superstructure to granite. By early 1885 architect Myers had submitted an amended design plan incorporating the change to hard stone, a change whose cost was estimated at $613,865.[16] Contractor Taylor was unwilling to incur these extra costs, particularly since the business depression of 1883–1885 had checked the sale to settlers of the three million acres of land awarded to his syndicate as payment for construction.[17]

While the controversy raged, work on the Capitol came to a halt during spring and summer 1885, but the building syndicate, faced with rising costs and impatient investors, could not afford to delay indefinitely. On July 16 Taylor agreed to construct the superstructure of granite, "provided the State will furnish me a granite quarry accessible and suitable for the building, free of cost, and furnish such number of convicts as I may require, not to exceed 1000, I to board, clothe and guard them."[18] He also stipulated that various structural changes be made to the building, in order to reduce its cost by at least $100,000, and that the time allowed for its completion be extended by three years. The Capitol Board quickly agreed to Taylor's propositions, a supplemental contract was drawn up on July 25, and up to five hundred convicts from state penitentiaries were assigned to the building syndicate, which was to pay sixty-five cents a day to cover the cost of feeding, clothing, and guarding them.[19] The convicts were put to work

---

[16] *Third Biennial Report of the Capitol Building Commission to the Governor of Texas*, Nov. 1, 1886 (Austin: Triplett and Hutchings, State Printers, 1886), 8. Later in 1885 Myers fell out with the building commissioners when they complained of nine defects in his plans. His refusal to submit modified plans or to meet with the Capitol Board led to the latter taking legal proceedings against him in 1886. The case was subsequently dropped, seemingly because of insufficient concrete evidence against Myers, but the rift was never healed. Rathjen, "The Texas State House," 449–452.

[17] If immigration to Texas had continued at the rate expected when the contract was awarded, the syndicate would have benefited richly. American *GCNJ*, IX (Aug., 1885), 2. See also Ruth Allen, "The Capitol Boycott: A Study in Peaceful Labor Tactics, 1885–1889," in *Chapters in the History of Organized Labor in Texas*, University of Texas Publication No. 4142, Nov. 15, 1941 (Austin: The University, 1941), 46. This paper draws not only on Allen's published work but also on many of the original sources used by Allen.

[18] *Third Biennial Report*, 33.

[19] *Reports of the Superintendent and Financial Agent of the Texas State Penitentiaries for two years ending October 31 1886*, in Allen, "The Capitol Boycott," 59. See also American *GCNJ*, XI (Aug., 1888), 3, and Crissey, "The Vanishing Range," 295.

in the granite quarries at Marble Falls, fifteen miles south of Burnet, and also constructed a narrow gauge railway from the quarries to join the Austin and Northwest railroad at Burnet. (The quarry owners had agreed to supply, free of charge, all the granite needed to construct the Capitol.) Shortly after these revised plans had been agreed, the Capitol syndicate sublet the contract for construction of the entire building to a young German-born builder, Gus Wilke of Chicago. Wilke had initially been employed in 1882 to put in the basement of the Capitol, and having accomplished this work satisfactorily, his contract was renewed and extended in 1885.

The problems that had plagued the Capitol project in its early stages were as nothing to the controversy that was to break over the use of convict labor. The opposition of public opinion in Texas was made clear in the many protests sent to the Capitol Board when the revised plans were announced.[20] But much more bitter and prolonged opposition came from the American Granite Cutters' Union. It had already opposed Wilke over the use of nonunion labor, and became even more enraged when its members' financial interests were threatened by the use of a convict work force.[21] Any collaboration in teaching convicts to cut granite would reduce the wages of skilled tradesmen and impede the union's efforts to achieve better conditions within the industry. These dangers were explained in the monthly circular of the Granite Cutters' Union in September 1885:

If 200 granite cutters work with, and teach 100 convicts the trade the probability is that in twelve months time there would be but 100 granite cutters and the number of convicts would be increased to 200, and in two years time there would be 300 convicts and no free granite cutters whatever employed on the job, for after the first lot is taught they will be put to teach other convicts, and thus drive out free labor altogether, for we have been reliably informed that the state officials of Texas have agreed to supply the contractors with 500 convicts.[22]

In December 1884 the Austin branch of the union had fixed the wage rate for its members working on the Capitol project at $4.00 per day, but Wilke subsequently offered only from $2.75 to $3.00, and only if these terms were accepted would he cease employing convicts. But his conditions were unacceptable to the Granite Cutters' Union, which was further angered by a letter from Wilke to the union, in which he had

---

[20] *Third Biennial Report*, 34.

[21] Granite Cutters' International Association of America to Ben Owens, Aug. 29, 1938, Capitol Syndicate Case Correspondence, Labor Movement in Texas Papers (Eugene C. Barker Texas History Center, University of Texas, Austin).

[22] Quoted in ibid.

threatened to "hire any good mechanic whether he be a scab as you call it or not. I will not permit you, nor any society, to dictate whom I shall employ, whether they be convicts or free labor."[23] The union voted unanimously to boycott the Capitol project, and a circular to this effect was published in Austin in December 1885, warning cutters to keep away until Wilke had stopped hiring convict labor:

Granite Cutters of America, show . . . Gus Wilke and his employers . . . that free men will not submit to the introduction of slavery into our trade under the . guise of contract convict labor, and that you will not teach convicts our trade to enrich these schemers, who care for nothing but the almighty dollar and now seek to degrade our trade to fill their own pockets.[24]

The union's injunction was not universally obeyed, according to the Graniteville (Missouri) branch secretary, who declared in the *Granite Cutters' National Journal* in February 1886:

Regarding the Austin job I [am] informed that there are a few of the brotherhood (although they are unworthy of the name now) working there at a bill of prices far below the Austin bill of prices. They have no shed, but Wilkie [*sic*] has fixed up an eight-foot fence with a line of barbed wire against the top of it, and no one is allowed inside but the workmen. Think of Gus Wilkie's fine promises when he is paying such a low bill of prices as will drive all his scabs out from his barbed wire fence as soon as spring comes, and what will they do then, poor things, as their names are all known and will soon be published for the information of square men.

The citizens of Burnet are indignant at the way Wilkie is acting, as they have subscribed about $1,500 and gave him [this] on his guarantee that the stone would all be cut there by free labor. They are expressing their opinions about Gus Wilkie and very hard words, but as is well known, hard words have no effect on him as long as he can get tools and fools to do his bidding.[25]

On the whole, however, the boycott was well supported, and soon caused Wilke to look abroad in search of the required skilled labor that the American union refused to supply. In April 1886 he sent his agent George Berry to Aberdeen in order to recruit 150 granite cutters and fifteen blacksmiths to complete the construction of the Capitol. For his services Berry was allegedly paid $600 and promised promotion to the post of an assistant foreman in the Burnet granite yard.[26] He first ad-

[23] Quoted in ibid.

[24] Austin *Daily Statesman*, Dec. 10, 1885.

[25] Quoted in Granite Cutters' International Association of America to Ben Owens, Aug. 29, 1938.

[26] American *GCNJ*, X (May, 1886), quoted in ibid. See also payroll vouchers of stonecutters employed by Gus Wilke, May–July 1886, in which Berry is listed as an assistant foreman at Burnet, earning forty cents per hour. Records of the Capitol Building Commission, RG AO1 2-10/444, folder 1, voucher 12; folder 2, voucher 16; folder 3, voucher 17 (Archives Division, Texas State Library, Austin; cited hereafter as TSL).

Up to 500 convicts from Texas state penitentiaries were assigned to the Capitol building syndicate and employed as granite cutters in the quarries at Marble Falls, Texas. *Courtesy Austin History Center, Austin Public Library.*

vertised his requirements in the Aberdeen press, then on April 12 organized a meeting in the Northern Friendly Society Hall in the city.[27] This gathering attracted an audience of 300, of whom 120 had already been recruited to go to Austin as a result of the earlier newspaper advertisement. The purpose of the meeting was to give particulars of the expedition to these recruits, as well as to invite applications for the remaining vacancies. Builder Robert Hall, presiding, drew on his own experience of four years spent in the U.S.A. to recommend the venture, particularly in view of the depression through which he said the Aberdeen granite trade was then passing.[28] Details of wages and working conditions were explained by a Mr. Prescott of London, representing Gus Wilke. The recruits were promised at least eighteen months'

---

[27] Aberdeen *Daily Free Press*, Apr. 3, 1886.

[28] He claimed that times had not been so bad in Aberdeen for twenty years and believed that by going to Austin, the emigrants would benefit not only themselves, but also their fellow workmen who remained at home. (Aberdeen *Journal*, Apr. 13, 1886). See also Aberdeen *Evening Express*, Apr. 12, 1886, and Aberdeen *Evening Gazette*, Apr. 13, 1886, for further details on this meeting. It seems that he may ultimately have followed his own advice, for a Robert Hall is listed on three payroll vouchers of stonecutters employed at Burnet, in March, April, and May 1887. Records of the Capitol Building Commission, RG AO1 2-10/445, folder 2, voucher 11; folder 5, voucher 2; RG AO1 2-10/446, folder 1, voucher 2 (TSL).

steady employment at wages of $4 to $6 per day, board and lodging at only $16 to $20 per month, and prepayment of a proportion or the whole of the £10 fare.[29] Single men were to repay this advance out of their first month's wages, but married men were allowed to defer repayment until the second or third month. Recruits were required to prove their commitment to the bargain by paying "earnest money" of twenty-five shillings each, whereupon they were issued with their sailing tickets.[30]

Approximately eighty-six recruits left Aberdeen with Berry on April 15 on the first stage of an eighteen-day journey to Austin, embarking the following day on the Anchor liner *Circassia* at Greenock.[31] Under the original agreement they were to have been shipped direct to Galveston, Texas, but when Wilke found it was not only cheaper but also safer—from his point of view—to have them transported by coastal steamer to Norfolk, Virginia, and thence by train to Texas, the initial

---

[29] Although the men were engaged initially for only eighteen months, it was expected that their contracts would be renewed, as construction of the Capitol was expected to take another four years. Aberdeen *Evening Gazette*, Apr. 15, 1886.

[30] A dispute arose when two blacksmiths, having paid this sum, were then told their services were not required, since Berry had been unable to obtain his full complement of stonecutters. The two blacksmiths complained to the sheriff that they had been defrauded, whereupon Berry was arrested and held in custody for a short time until he had paid a fine of ten pounds. House Misc. Doc. No. 572, 50th Cong., 1st Sess., p. 146.

[31] There is confusion over the exact number of recruits who left Aberdeen on April 15 and also over the number subsequently employed at Austin. Although the Aberdeen *Evening Gazette* had stated on April 13 that over 120 men had taken up Berry's offer, both this newspaper and the Aberdeen *Daily Free Press* reported on April 15 that the party leaving Aberdeen had consisted of seventy-eight masons and seven blacksmiths, a total of eighty-five men. Perhaps some men were rejected as unsuitable after having been engaged, but other sources indicate further inconsistencies. The Aberdeen *Journal* (Apr. 16, 1886) reported that ninety men had left Aberdeen with Berry though, according to the Glasgow *Weekly Mail* (Apr. 17, 1886) only eighty-seven arrived at Greenock to embark on the *Circassia*. In May 1886 the American *GCNJ* stated that eighty-six men (seventy-eight cutters and eight blacksmiths) had arrived on the *Circassia*, a figure corroborated later by the Aberdeen *Journal* (May 17, 1886) when it published a letter of thanks sent to the Anchor Line agents by three masons on behalf of the eighty-six men who had left Aberdeen. Meanwhile, the New York *Herald* (April 26) had reported the arrival of only seventy-five stonecutters on the *Circassia* (article quoted in the Aberdeen *Evening Gazette*, May 10). This total may have discounted the blacksmiths, and the general accuracy of the *Herald*'s account is open to question, for it stated that the men had been recruited in Glasgow to work for Wilke on the construction of a State Capitol at Topeka, Kansas.

If we accept that eighty-six recruits arrived in the U.S.A., then, subtracting the twenty-four men who (according to the American *GCNJ*) stayed at New York, a total of sixty-two men should have proceeded to Texas. The Capitol payroll vouchers for May 1886 do indeed list the names of sixty-two Scottish employees (fifty-six cutters and six blacksmiths) but a list of Scottish recruits published by the American *GCNJ*, also in May, contains sixty-four names. Four names that appear on the May payroll do not appear in the American *GCNJ* list (Alex Milne, Alex Moir, John Smith, and Alex Warrender). The first two names may have been wrongly transcribed on the American *GCNJ* list as James Milne and Alex Moore, but four other names included on this list do not appear on the May payroll (David Dawson, Sr., James Duthie, George Findlay, and James McAlpine). David Dawson, Sr., is listed among the blacksmiths on the June payroll, and by July 1886 there were seventy-five Scots on the payroll. Two of the original recruits had died by that time, and the increase is explained by the arrival of the second batch of fifteen workmen who left Aberdeen on June 17.

port of landing was changed to New York.[32] On April 17 the Glasgow *Weekly Mail* reported (somewhat inaccurately as regards the emigrants' destination and employment) that

On Thursday afternoon 87 tradesmen arrived at Greenock by special train from Aberdeen. . . . The men include granite cutters and builders, who have been engaged on an 18 months' agreement to work at 4 dollars per day, in Texas, at the erection of the Court house in Galveston. The men state that their passage is to be paid out and home, and that they have a guarantee from a firm of standing in Aberdeen that they were not going out to work regarding which there is a dispute between contractors and workmen.[33]

Berry had thus neglected to tell his recruits that the need for their importation had arisen because of the boycott of the Austin contract by American native labor. He had admitted that convict labor was employed on the project, but declared that this had come about only because insufficient free labor was available in the U.S.A., and promised that once Wilke had secured the required number of free workers he would cease to employ prisoners.[34] Given their limited understanding of the true state of affairs, it is likely that the Aberdeen recruits were totally unprepared for the reception given them on arriving at New York.

Informed by telegram of the embarkation of Berry and his recruits, three officials of the Granite Cutters' Union were sent to New York to intercept the party. In particular, they hoped to secure Berry's arrest for importing workers into the U.S.A. in violation of the Alien Contract Labor Law. Initial attempts to persuade the U.S. District Attorney at New York to have Berry arrested under this law failed for lack of immediate proof that a contract had in fact been made with the immigrants, but the union officials did manage to persuade twenty-four of the recruits not to proceed to Texas.

On returning to Castle Garden and going amongst the men and explaining matters, 24 of them decided not to go any further with Berry; but he, with the assistance of two ruffians, named Thom and Dawson, coaxed and coerced the remainder aboard the ferry-boat for the New Jersey side. Berry and his assistants dragged some of them in such a manner that the U.S. Deputy Marshal dared them to lay a finger on any of them or he would arrest them for assault and battery.[35]

While these men were boarding the steamer *Comal* for Newport News, Virginia, two of the American union representatives had discov-

---

[32] American *GCNJ*, X (June, 1886), 3.

[33] Ibid., 2; Glasgow *Weekly Mail*, Apr. 17, 1886.

[34] House Misc. Doc. No. 572, 50th Cong., 1st Sess., p. 146: evidence of David Dawson.

[35] American *GCNJ*, X (May, 1886), 3.

ered from the men who remained in New York that the recruits had in fact been given printed contracts by Berry, which, when they were shown to immigration officials at Castle Garden, were said to be in clear violation of the Contract Labor Law. The three documents in their possession covered the conditions of their employment, accommodation, and the prepayment of their passages, and included two certificates from Gus Wilke. One of these stated that he had authorized Berry to engage and bring to Austin the granite cutters and blacksmiths required to work on the State Capitol, and stipulated that "the fare for passage advanced by me is expected to be returned, out of earnings made by cutting."[36] His other certificate gave details of the wages and accommodation to be provided for the recruits at Burnet, while the third document, a ticket issued by the Anchor Line, gave proof of the prepayment of passage as far as Galveston. When these documents were put before the district attorney, along with the affidavits of two renegade recruits (Charles Falconer and Robert Maitland), he admitted that Wilke was in breach of the law, and so the way was cleared for the American Granite Cutters' Union to initiate the prosecution of Wilke and the syndicate he represented.

Having supplied the American union with ample proof of the existence of printed contracts, the renegade recruits, with that union's blessing, sought clean jobs in the granite centers of the East, ten ultimately finding work in Vermont.[37] Meanwhile, the tradesmen who had elected to proceed to Texas arrived at Burnet on May 2, the union's attempts to head them off at Norfolk and Galveston having failed. In order to avoid confrontation, they had disembarked quietly at Newport News, from where they had traveled by train, first to Houston, and then to Austin. A telegram intimating their safe arrival was despatched by four of the men and appeared in the Aberdeen *Daily Free Press* on May 8. It made no reference to the substantial depletion of the party at New York, but merely stated that the men had "arrived all safe, and find the job everything as represented."[38] An eyewitness at Houston had described them as a "hardy and robust set of men, with plenty of bone and muscle," whose arrival had given him "the best evidence I have yet had that the capitol would be completed."[39] As the Austin *Daily Statesman* pointed out later, the recruits were not paupers, "but on

[36] Wilke's [undated] Letter of Introduction for George Berry while in Aberdeen (Federal Court Records, Austin), in Allen, "The Capitol Boycott," 57 (quotation).

[37] American *GCNJ*, XI (Aug., 1888), 3; House Misc. Doc. No. 572, 50th Cong., 1st Sess., p. 143: evidence of Josiah Dyer.

[38] David Dawson, George T. Kelman, Thomas Kesson, and William R. Thom. Aberdeen *Daily Free Press*, May 8, 1886.

[39] Galveston *Daily News*, May 4, 1886.

the contrary are skilled artisans, evidently capable of paying their way anywhere . . . they came of their own motion . . . are paid the very highest price for their labor . . . and are satisfied."[40]

One of the recruits, granite cutter Alexander Greig, writing home to his parents on May 3, spoke of the hearty welcome the party had received in Texas and refuted claims that they had been deceived. He painted a different picture of the New York incident from that described in the *Granite Cutters' National Journal*, which alleged that the men had been forced to continue and had been manhandled aboard the ferryboat.[41] In Greig's words:

> While we were at New York, there were several of the society met us, and tried all that was in their power to get us to stop at New York; and I am sorry to say that there was a few fools amongst us who listened to what they had to say, and stayed behind to their sorrow and shame, and there was a report got into the New York newspapers which said that we were detained in New York, and that Mr. Berry was arrested, and Mr. Wilkie [*sic*] fined a hundred dollars, which is the biggest falsehood that ever went into any newspaper. You can tell anybody that asks about us that everything is right, and that we have been treated well. I was told that I was growing fat upon it. I am first-class in health and intend to stick in. This is the most splendid country I have ever seen. I have seen nothing to equal it through all the States.[42]

But not all the recruits were of the same mind, particularly once work had actually begun. Perhaps Greig too became disillusioned, for his promise in his first letter that he would send home a weekly diary to his parents did not materialize.[43] According to the Galveston *Daily News* of May 13, many of the men, already angry at the expense incurred during their unexpected seven-day journey from New York, were soon disappointed in their expectations of high wages. It estimated that about half the recruits had had no previous experience of granite cutting, and were unable to earn even a dollar a day. In fact, the payroll vouchers for the period May 1886 to May 1887 indicate that the stonecutters earned an average wage of twenty-seven cents per hour, though individual payments varied from only four cents to fifty cents per hour.[44] The blacksmiths were paid forty cents per hour, though the

[40] Austin *Daily Statesman*, July 14, 1886.

[41] See this article, p. 476. The men singled out by the *GCNJ* for criticism for coercing recruits to proceed to Texas, Dawson and Thom, were later involved in sending the telegram to Aberdeen intimating the party's safe arrival. American *GCNJ*, X (May, 1886), 3.

[42] Aberdeen *Evening Gazette*. May 17, 1886.

[43] At any rate, no letters from Greig were subsequently published in the Aberdeen *Evening Gazette* during the rest of 1886. His promise to send home a weekly diary was noted in American *GCNJ*, X (June, 1886), which also quotes his initial May 3 letter.

[44] Galveston *Daily News*, May 13, 1886; Records of the Capitol Building Commission, RG AO1 2 10/444–446 (TSL). See also affidavit of Alexander Gibb (case 2061) quoted in Capitol Syndi-

Galveston *Daily News* (May 13) alleged that these men, employed as tool sharpeners, were particularly inept. Genuine granite cutters on piece work therefore became impatient at time and money unnecessarily lost in waiting for their implements to be sharpened. Most of the men were accommodated and employed at "Wilkeville," a fenced enclosure on the southeast side of Burnet adjacent to the railway line. All but two recruits were initially boarded at a monthly charge of approximately seventeen dollars each. After May 1886, however, only a few Scots were billed for accommodation, and in September 1886 and March 1887 no deductions were made for board. According to the Galveston *Daily News,* the Scots soon became dissatisfied with their working conditions and accommodation:

Bitter feelings and homesickness are cropping out everywhere. Working out in the sun with the thermometer standing at 80 or 90°, and four to six men packed in a lodging room, ten feet square, along with indifferent food, is something that was not calculated on.[45]

This view was corroborated three months later in a circular issued by the Austin Assembly of the Knights of Labor, which alleged (in direct contradiction of the claims made by the Austin *Daily Statesman*) that "The work is hard, and prices and wages low, and as a consequence the stone cutters are leaving and seeking employment in other places."[46] By the end of October 1886 at least three of the Scots had died, and by May 1887 the payroll vouchers show that only fifteen of the original recruits were still employed at Burnet.[47] It had soon become evident that Wilke had no intention of keeping his promise to diminish the convict labor force once he had secured sufficient free labor. On the contrary, he almost doubled the number of convicts employed, according to one Aberdeen recruit, blacksmith David Dawson, who left the job

---

cate Case Correspondence, Labor Movement in Texas Papers. Gibb claimed that during his employment at Burnet he had sometimes made $80 a month by piece work.

[45] Galveston *Daily News,* May 13, 1886, quoted in American *GCNJ,* X (June, 1886), 3. Almost two years earlier, in August 1884, Wilke had advertised in the *GCNJ* for thirty cutters to work on the Capitol project. But the following month a notice from H. Z. A. Laporte, secretary of the Austin branch of the union, warned members against believing Wilke's promises of well-paid, steady work in a good climate (Allen, "The Capitol Boycott," 46–47). Some men may have been sent on to the granite quarry at Marble Falls. According to the American *GCNJ* of May 1886, the Aberdeen contingent had found insufficient stone to cut at Burnet on their arrival and some of them had been sent on to the quarry to work with the convicts. See Capitol Syndicate Case Correspondence, Labor Movement in Texas Papers.

[46] Circular from J. Geggie, Chairman, Committee, Capitol Assembly No. 2182, Knights of Labor, quoted in the Austin *Daily Statesman,* Aug. 11, 1886. But an editorial in this paper the following day criticized Geggie for his "hounding and persecuting of innocent men" and declared that "this boycotting business must be broken up."

[47] They were George Mutch (23), died June 13; John Smith (27), drowned June 27; and George Moir (22), died October 15. Before the Scots dispersed, they commemorated these deaths by preparing and erecting a granite memorial in the cemetery at Burnet.

early and who subsequently testified to Wilke's misdemeanors before
the Congressional Enquiry into violations of the Contract Labor Law in
1888.[48] According to the Austin *Daily Statesman* of July 23, 1886, Wilke
at that time had 200 convicts employed at quarrying and 100 at cutting
stone, in addition to 148 "free" stonecutters, making a total of 448 men
at work in Marble Falls and Burnet preparing granite for use in Austin.
By October 5 the number of convicts employed had risen to 350, and
the newspaper predicted that by the following April all the rock required for the Capitol would have been quarried.

Before disillusionment set in, David Dawson had, at Wilke's request
and on his behalf, secured a further contingent of Aberdonians to go to
Austin, perhaps to replace those who had defected at New York.[49]
Dawson contacted a friend in Aberdeen, granite merchant John Petrie,
who then advertised in the Aberdeen *Journal* for thirty cutters and two
masons to go to Austin.[50] As a result of his appeal, fifteen extra recruits
left Aberdeen on June 17 to embark on the Anchor liner *Turnissa* at
Glasgow.[51] Wilke subsequently paid Petrie $15.60 for his services, but
did not make use of him again, for when more stonecutting vacancies
at Austin were advertised in the Aberdeen *Journal* on October 9, interested parties were told to apply to the newspaper office, not to Petrie.
Work on the Capitol proceeded quickly during 1886 and 1887: by November 1886 Wilke's monthly payroll was almost $50,000, and by the
following summer the walls and most ornamental work were finished,
and the dome was taking shape.[52] The Aberdeen recruits' work was
coming to an end, and many of them were preparing to leave Texas.

Meanwhile, however, the American Granite Cutters' Union was pur-
suing the prosecution of the Capitol syndicate through the Austin
courts. Papers provided by the renegade recruits at New York, which
clearly indicated the existence of an illegal contract involving Wilke,
Berry, and the immigrants, were forwarded to Austin. In July 1886
Wilke, the Farwell Brothers, Taylor, and Babcock were accordingly in-
dicted in the Federal District Court in Austin, charged with having violated the one-year-old Contract Labor Law. Hearing of the case was
postponed until August 1887, and during the interval the union cam-

---

[48] House Misc. Doc. No. 572, 50th Cong., 1st Sess., p. 146. Dawson, who was self-employed in
1886, had gone out on the strength of Berry's promise that blacksmiths could earn $4 per day,
and he had selected the other Aberdeen blacksmiths on Berry's behalf.

[49] Aberdeen *Evening Gazette*, July 12, 1886; Austin *Daily Statesman*, July 23, 1886.

[50] Aberdeen *Journal*, June 1, 1886 (advertisement for thirty cutters and two blacksmiths);
Ibid., June 11, 1886 (advertisement for a few more stonecutters).

[51] Aberdeen *Evening Gazette*, June 17, 1886; Aberdeen *Journal*, June 18, 1886. Their passages
were arranged by Aberdeen shipping agents John Sheed and Company. See also American
GCNJ, X (July, 1886), 1; and ibid., XI (Aug., 1888), 3.

[52] Rathjen, "The Texas State House," 454.

The Aberdeen recruits soon discovered that the high wages and utopian working conditions promised by Berry did not materialize, and dissatisfaction rapidly set in. *Courtesy Austin History Center, Austin Public Library.*

paigned for funds to finance its prosecution, securing a grant of $5,000 from the General Assembly of the Knights of Labor.[53] In March 1887 several Aberdeen recruits who expected to leave Austin before August testified on behalf of the prosecution before a Circuit Court clerk in Austin. They included George Edwards, Alexander Gregg, and James Taylor, who all intended to return to Aberdeen, Thomas Kesson from Stonehaven (bound for Georgia), Alexander Gibbs from Aberdeen (going to St. Louis), Alexander Steel from Wartle (also going to Missouri in the hope of finding work at St. Louis or Graniteville) and William Porter, one of the blacksmiths (going to Wisconsin). George Kelman, who had been in the U.S.A. on four previous occasions, hoped to find work in Texas. All the witnesses claimed that they had come to Austin on the strength of a promise of employment made to them by George Berry in Aberdeen in April 1886. Berry had shown them a letter from Gus Wilke authorizing him to recruit 150 granite cutters, whose passage money would be prepaid on condition that they subsequently repaid the sums advanced ($38–$40) out of their wages. According to Alexander Steele:

George Berry told me all about the job and about the climate, and about there being good water here and that there was shade going to be put up, and that Gus Wilke had a steam traveler that there was labourers there to turn those rocks and that we would have a big pile of rocks there which we would never have to wait for and that the quarry was fifteen miles distant and that there was a large number of convicts there some quarrying and some cutting rock and that if we would agree to come with him our passage money would be advanced all excepting one pound five shillings, which we had to pay part of it as a security that we would come when the expedition started and part of the money went for our ship kit and to transfer our baggage from Greenock station to the boat. Also that it would require at least 18 months steady granite cutting to complete cutting stone for the building and that we had to pay back our advanced fares . . . I asked him [Berry] why the job was scabbed and he told me that the National Granite Cutters Union scabbed the job unjustly and that it was scabbed nearly three months before they commenced to cut rock, or before there was convicts employed but that the convicts would be discharged when we arrived at Burnet, Texas, and that was the only fault the Stone Cutters Union had against it, and that we could get board and lodging from 16 to 18 and 20 dollars per month.[54]

---

[53] Allen, "The Capitol Boycott," 51.

[54] Cross examination of Alexander C. Steele in the Circuit Court of the United States, Western District of Texas, at Austin, Mar. 24, 1887, case no. 2082, in Allen, "The Capitol Boycott," 71 (quotation). See also Capitol Syndicate Case Correspondence, Labor Movement in Texas Papers, for similar testimony given by three recruits (William Chalmers, Alexander Duncan, and James Milne) who had gone to St. George, Maine, instead of proceeding to Texas.

On this basis the men had made verbal agreements with Berry to work for Wilke (whom they first met in Houston on May 2). But on July 30, 1886, those still at Burnet were asked to sign a statement to the effect that they had made "no contract of any character whatsoever with Gus Wilke or with any other person for Gus Wilke to perform any service . . . for Wilke previous to . . . becoming a resident of the USA."[55] In their testimony Steele and another witness, Andrew Durno, both admitted that they had signed this document knowing it to be false. Durno had been ill at the time and Steele had feared that refusal to sign would have meant dismissal and great hardship; "at that time I was without money and understood from others in the public papers that every union and trade organization wanted to see us starve."[56]

Hearing of the case was again postponed in August 1887, and when it eventually came to court two years later Wilke stood alone, the names of the members of the Capitol Syndicate having been dropped from the prosecution.[57] Wilke admitted the charge of violating the Contract Labor Law and was fined the statutory penalty of $1,000 for each illegally imported worker, together with $1,000 costs, making a total penalty of $64,000. But he was given up to eighteen months' stay of execution in order to appeal to Washington, and when judgment was finally executed in 1893 he was fined only $8,000 and costs. This clemency infuriated the Granite Cutters' Union, which claimed that Wilke had pleaded guilty in order to shield the Capitol Syndicate, and that the syndicate had then used its political influence in Washington to nullify the sentence passed on its scapegoat and thus defeat the law.[58]

The American Granite Cutters' Union was interested not only in prosecuting the contractors but in punishing the Aberdeen tradesmen who had worked at Burnet, and throughout 1886 it mounted a sustained attack on them through its trade journal. The action of the

---

[55] Statement of workmen at Burnet Quarry, July 30, 1886, Federal Court Records, Austin. In fact, in his evidence to the Circuit Court clerk George Edwards had denied having made a contract with Berry to work for Wilke before leaving Scotland.

[56] Cross examination of Alexander C. Steele (case no. 2082) and testimony of Andrew Durno (case no. 2051) in the Circuit Court of the United States, Western District of Texas, at Austin, Mar. 24, 1887, in Allen, "The Capitol Boycott," 75, 80.

[57] On the District Attorney's motion to drop charges against the Farwell Brothers and Amos Babcock. Allen, "The Capitol Boycott," 51.

[58] Why, for instance, did a North Dakota senator with no obvious interest in the case request the district attorney at Austin to grant a stay of execution on his judgment against Wilke? See Federal Court, Austin District, letter of Aug. 29, 1890, from F. A. Reeve, Acting Solicitor, U.S. Department of Justice, to A. J. Evans, U.S. District Attorney, Austin District, authorizing a stay of execution on the judgment against Wilke at the request of Senator G. A. Pierce of North Dakota, in Allen, "The Capitol Boycott," 82. See also American Federation of Labor, Convention Proceedings, 1889, pp. 24–25, in ibid., 85–86. The Granite Cutters' Union persuaded the American Federation of Labor to protest to President Harrison against what it saw as an evasion of the law.

strikebreakers was condemned as "despicable" at a time when the union was striving to secure higher wages and shorter hours within the granite industry,[59] though one correspondent did observe that the ill wind that had blown the Scots to Texas had at least relieved Aberdeen of the dregs of its granite workers.[60] A circular issued by the Austin Assembly of the Knights of Labor in August 1886 published the names of the strikebreakers with the warning

Mark these men, Knights of Labor, and union men of all classes. Do not work with them and have no dealings with them whatever. It is only by uniting that we can stop the working of convicts on public works. Men who work on jobs with convicts ought to be blacklisted, as they are no good to any job.

If any of these men, or men who say they have been working on the capitol building at Austin, or at Burnet or Oatmanville, come near you, let them take a walk; give them no work, and see that they get no work in your neighborhood.[61]

When the Austin contract ended in summer 1887, and the workmen prepared to disperse throughout the U.S.A., the *Granite Cutters' National Journal* reissued the list of Aberdeen recruits, along with the names of other strikebreakers not recruited by George Berry. This was again done in the hope that any of these men who sought work in other American granite centers would be remembered and cold-shouldered by the union.[62]

While it is not known what became of the blacklisted labor force, Wilke and Berry both made their peace with the Granite Cutters' Union in 1890, on payment of a penalty of a mere $500 each imposed by the union before it would deal with them again.[63] Perhaps the protracted litigation and opposition of powerful business and political leaders had simply proved too much for the union, exhausting its funds and forcing it to drop its prosecution of the syndicate. The union certainly regarded its achievement as a rather hollow, cosmetic victory, for it had always maintained that Wilke was just the agent of the much more powerful Capitol Syndicate, and it felt that failure to secure the conviction of the syndicate itself really constituted defeat.[64]

---

[59] American *GCNJ*, X (June, 1886), 1.

[60] Ibid., X (Aug., 1886), 5. William McQueen, union branch secretary at Milford, Massachusetts, declared that the men who accompanied Berry were all "bums and scabs," who had been unable to prosper in Aberdeen and who would therefore also fail in Burnet.

[61] Austin *Daily Statesman*, Aug. 11, 1886; Circular from J. Geggie, Chairman, Committee, Capitol Assembly No. 2182, Knights of Labor, quoted in Allen, "The Capitol Boycott," 84.

[62] American *GCNJ*, XI (June, 1887), 4–5.

[63] Allen, "The Capitol Boycott," 54.

[64] Ibid. See also San Antonio *Daily Express*, Aug. 2, 1888, which published a declaration by Abner Taylor that, though he had opposed the importation of the Scottish stonecutters, neither he nor any other member of the Syndicate had had the authority to prevent it.

Nevertheless, the ramifications of the Capitol boycott extended beyond Texas and beyond the confines of the Granite Cutters' Union, to Washington itself. Since the incident provided the first real test of the Contract Labor Law, it attracted national attention and was largely responsible for an enquiry by a committee of the House of Representatives into violations of this legislation. The committee began its hearings in July 1888 (over a year before the case against Wilke finally came to trial) and the activities of the Capitol Syndicate were included in its lengthy investigations. Testimony against the contractors was led by Josiah Dyer, an English immigrant and secretary of the American Granite Cutters' Union since 1877. In "support of his claim that the Aberdeen tradesmen had been imported illegally under contract, he produced affidavits from four recruits, two of whom had left the party at New York and had not proceeded to Texas."[65] Their written evidence was corroborated by two more recruits who appeared before the enquiry in person. James Anderson (who had left the party at New York) and David Dawson (who in June 1886 had acted as Wilke's agent in importing a further batch of Aberdeen tradesmen) had both since found lucrative employment in Vermont and had no intention of returning to Scotland.[66]

Meanwhile in Austin the troubles that had plagued the construction of the Capitol since its inception were not yet over. Building costs had doubled from the original estimate of $1,500,000 to $3,000,000.[67] In 1887, drastic alterations had to be made to the design of the half-built dome, when it became clear that the original structure was likely to be dangerously heavy. Following the dedication of the Capitol on May 18, 1888, a gala and ball were under way inside the new building, when the celebrations were (quite literally) dampened by the roof leaking during a rainstorm. Allegations by W. P. Hardeman, the superintendent of building and grounds, that there were major structural defects in the roof and drains, were hotly denied by the building commissioners and the contractors.[68] In August 1888 contractor Abner Taylor and sub-

---

[65] The affidavits of Charles Falconer and Robert Maitland had originally been produced before the district attorney at New York in 1886, in order to allow the Granite Cutters' Union to take legal action against Wilke. See this article, p. 13. Their affidavits were presented to the Congressional Enquiry in 1888, along with those of William Dickie and Hugh Munroe, who had carried on to Texas and had worked at Burnet. House Misc. Doc. No. 572, 50th Cong., 1st Sess., pp. 139–140, 148, 151 (quotation).

[66] Ibid., 146–151. Dawson had returned temporarily to Scotland, but had now brought his wife and family to the U.S.A. and was working in Barre at $2.75 per day, making four times the wage he estimated he could earn in Scotland. Anderson, who was earning a similar wage, had taken out naturalization papers with the intention of becoming an American citizen.

[67] Crissey, "The Vanishing Range," 295.

[68] Rathjen, "The Texas State House," 458–459. The commissioners claimed that Hardeman was unfamiliar with the specifications and was therefore not competent to judge the structure.

contractor Gus Wilke tendered the building for acceptance and asked for the final settlement of their account; but Hardeman enlisted the support of the state's attorney general, Jim Hogg, to ensure that payment of the residue of the land due to the contractors would be withheld until all defects had been repaired to his satisfaction.[69] Taylor, desperate to conclude the contract, offered to have independent experts inspect the building and promised to correct any faults that were pointed out to him. The Capitol Board accordingly secured the services of Washington architect Edward Miller, who examined the structure and reported a number of problems of a fairly minor nature. By December 1888 these faults had been rectified to Miller's satisfaction, and on December 8, on his recommendation, the state unanimously agreed to accept the building, thus closing the first troubled chapter in the history of the Texas State Capitol.

What was the main significance of the Capitol boycott of 1886 and the consequent introduction of strikebreakers from Aberdeen? The importation of the Scottish tradesmen did not hinder the completion of the building; indeed their skills, together with the continuing labor of numerous convicts, perhaps expedited its construction. Nor did the ill-feeling generated have any permanent impact on the continuing flow of granite tradesmen from northeast Scotland to the United States. The American Granite Cutters' Union certainly used the incident to make a stand against unfair competition from convict and nonunion labor. But its real significance lay in the way in which (through the ensuing court case and congressional enquiry) the dispute focused national attention on the one-year-old Contract Labor Law and exposed the inadequacy of that legislation.[70] The Capitol boycott provided the first test for legislation that, despite being rewritten by Congress on at least six occasions between 1887 and 1907, remained founded on a misconception and therefore never succeeded in its aim of preventing the immigration of undesirable aliens.

Wilke pointed out to the Capitol Board that he had warned of problems with a copper roof, but having registered his protest, he had then used the materials specified in the contract. Although he insisted he was not to blame for the defective roof, he felt that any fault in the structure would damage his reputation. For this reason, together with his desire to see the contract finally settled, he himself offered to bear the cost of either replacing the copper roof with a tin one, or guaranteeing to maintain the existing roof for a period of three years.

[69] American *GCNJ*, XI (May, 1888), 2; Ibid., XI (Aug., 1888), 1; Ibid., XI (Oct., 1888), 5.

[70] For instance, in the original act no provision was made for deporting offenders. This was amended in 1887, but until 1888 there were not inspectors at the ports to investigate violations of the law. Erickson, *American Industry and the European Immigrant,* 168–169.

The completed Capitol, seen here in an undated photograph, dominated the surrounding city. *Courtesy Prints and Photographs Collection, Center for American History, University of Texas at Austin.*

Figure 1. *David Crockett* by William Henry Huddle, 1889. Oil on canvas, 96 × 59 inches. *Courtesy Archives Division, Texas State Library.*

"The Hardy, Stalwart Son of Texas": Art and Mythology at the Capitol

EMILY FOURMY CUTRER*

WHEN THE NEW TEXAS CAPITOL WAS LITTLE MORE THAN A GLEAM IN the eye of its planners, discussion of its artistic embellishment had already commenced. Sometime during late 1881 or early 1882 Governor Oran M. Roberts summoned the German-American sculptor Elisabet Ney to Austin from her home in Waller County to meet with the Capitol Board and to make suggestions about the building's artistic program. A letter the sculptor later wrote to Roberts reveals the rather elaborate ideas the two shared. Both apparently had endorsed a plan calling for sculptural decoration on the building's interior and exterior. Four statues were to stand in the south vestibule just behind the main entrance; busts would ring the perimeter of the rotunda; and an elaborate frieze would ornament the main pediment above the Capitol's entrance. More significant than their ideas about medium and placement were the content and themes of their proposed art. In her letter, Ney called for statues and portrait busts "consecrated to the memory" of men who contributed "to the glory and elevation of the state," and she described the allegorical frieze as one "with representations of Advancing civilization triumphantly expelling barbarism: Indians, Buffaloes ceding the ground to the plow and domestique animals, and statesmanship, commerce, [and] science growing out of the context."[1]

With these prescriptions, the sculptor outlined an artistic program that undoubtedly would have struck a responsive chord not only with the Capitol Board, but also with much of its prospective Texas audience. It called for an art that was didactic as well as one that provided reinforcement for the culture's dominant ideologies of individualism,

*Emily Fourmy Cutrer, assistant professor of American studies at the University of Texas at Austin, is the author of *The Art of the Woman: The Life and Work of Elisabet Ney* (Lincoln: University of Nebraska Press, 1988).

[1]Elisabet Ney to Oran Roberts, Mar. 11, 1882, Oran Roberts Papers (Eugene C. Barker Texas History Center, University of Texas at Austin; cited hereafter as BTHC).

Manifest Destiny, and historical progress. While the sculptural program might have seemed too elaborate and expensive to the board, the content and themes of Ney's proposals nevertheless meshed well with the inherited values of Texas's late nineteenth-century leaders. Although the Capitol Board failed to endorse the specific plan proposed by Ney and Roberts, later legislatures, governors, and civic organizations would revive it in spirit. From the completion of the Capitol in 1888 through the early twentieth century, the state either appropriated funds or endorsed efforts of private organizations to provide art that espoused similar values for the interior and exterior of the building.[2]

The kind of art that eventually appeared in the Capitol was hardly unique to Texas, however; indeed, it is heir to nearly a century and a half of discussion about the place of art within a democratic society. As historian Neil Harris has pointed out, many of America's earliest leaders feared the development of a native tradition in the visual arts. To some eighteenth-century minds, particularly those descended from the Puritans, painting and sculpture represented the sophistication, luxury, and decadence they associated with monarchy and the Catholic Church and were pursuits that a nation hoping to nourish such virtues as restraint and simplicity might do well to avoid. Both aesthetic developments in Europe and national needs in the United States, however, provided answers to such objections and eventually demonstrated that art could in fact serve a democratic republic.[3]

In Europe, excavations of ancient artifacts at Pompeii and Herculaneum in the 1730s and 1740s, for example, had helped to arouse interest in antique objects, and the writings of numerous artists, critics, and historians had made others aware of the aesthetic possibilities of classical models. The resulting neoclassical style was concerned with more than formal and aesthetic qualities, however; it was, in effect, an artistic and architectural corollary to Enlightenment thought, which provided the intellectual underpinnings of the American Revolution. While philosophers wrote about an orderly, rational universe, neoclassical artists emphasized the importance of order, clarity, and emotional control. In the words of Johann Joachim Winckelmann, one of the most influential of the style's theoreticians, artists were to turn away from the frivolity and decorativeness of the baroque and rococo to work that expressed "a noble simplicity and a serene grandeur."[4]

---

[2] Ibid.; Austin *Daily Statesman*, Jan. 31, 1882.

[3] Neil Harris, *The Artist in American Society: The Formative Years, 1790–1860* (New York: George Braziller, 1966), 2–6.

[4] Hugh Honour, *Neo-classicism* (Middlesex: Penguin Books, 1968) is a helpful, and generally accurate, general discussion of the subject. For quotation, see p. 61.

For many painters, these qualities found their best expression in the depiction of ancient scenes; thus, closely related to the development of neoclassicism was the growing prominence of history painting. To Americans, the most important apologist for the genre was probably the Englishman Sir Joshua Reynolds, who in his *Discourses,* delivered between 1769 and 1790 at the Royal Academy, demanded that art serve a moral purpose by dealing with beauty and eternal truths. No genre was better equipped to do this, he believed, than a history painting that celebrated events in which human beings had proved themselves brave and noble. In order to avoid the trivial and temporal and thus to provide ethical guidance, Reynolds advised that artists choose subjects from ancient history. His contemporary, the American Benjamin West, however, offered an alternative.[5]

In 1771 in London West completed the *The Death of Wolfe,* a canvas that would have an enormous impact on the development of history painting not only in Europe, but also in America. Unlike many of his earlier works based on scenes from classical antiquity, this painting dealt with a recent historical event, the death of the British general James Wolfe at the battle of Quebec in 1759. Although many historians have focused on West's revolutionary use of contemporary costume and the sensation this innovation caused, an even more significant aspect of the painting was the way in which it elevated contemporary material to the moral level of antiquity and underscored the didactic possibilities of current events. By depicting a battle that had provided a focus for growing British nationalism and self-esteem, West demonstrated how history and art could serve national ends.[6]

The lesson was not lost on American artists or their public. During the Revolutionary War, John Adams, who feared the potentially corrupting influence of art, insisted that painters and sculptors nevertheless could perform a valuable service by "perpetuating to Posterity, the horrid deeds of our Enemies." One painter who took up the assignment, John Trumbull, also helped forge a national identity with his depictions of historic events such as the signing of the Declaration of Independence. At the same time, his contemporary Charles Willson Peale extended the definition of history painting by creating a virtual Pantheon of revolutionary leaders when he displayed their portraits in his gallery in Philadelphia. Unlike portraits commissioned by the wealthy

---

[5] Joshua Reynolds, *Discourses on Art,* ed. Robert R. Wark (New Haven: Yale University Press, 1975).

[6] Dennis Montagna, "Benjamin West's *The Death of General Wolfe:* A Nationalist Narrative," *American Art Journal,* XIII (Spring, 1981), 72–88.

for display in their own homes, Peale's canvases were hung in a public place and were intended to provide their audience with moral lessons about the nobility and inherent dignity of the individual, ideals he emphasized by generally depicting his subjects as straightforwardly as possible in pose, dress, and mood.[7]

Painters such as Trumbull and Peale, as well as many of their contemporaries and heirs among nineteenth-century artists, thus borrowed from and transformed European ideas to create a tradition of public art in the United States that, whatever its style or quality, had three general characteristics. First, it assumed that the function of art was to instruct and uplift; second, it emphasized the primary importance of public figures and events; and third, it reinforced or prescribed a set of values identified with the prevailing culture. In addition, American public art, like that of other nations, found its most widespread expression during periods of cultural stress or dislocation. During the late eighteenth and early nineteenth centuries, for example, it provided the U.S. with heroes and symbols that were intended to focus the country's growing sense of nationalism. After the Civil War, public art helped, on the one hand, to reconstruct that national identity, while on the other, it aided southerners in preserving a regional culture. Its function in Texas was similar. Historic and didactic in nature, the art in the Texas statehouse not only conforms to the social and cultural values of the state's dominant Anglo-American culture, but also is a means of perpetuating that culture through the construction of a specifically Texan mythology.

Just what that mythology is becomes apparent when one enters the Capitol from the south and confronts the four major works of art in the front foyer. On the east wall hangs William Henry Huddle's portrait of Davy Crockett, and on the west his depiction of the surrender of General Antonio López de Santa Anna. Two statues, portraits of Sam Houston and Stephen F. Austin by Elisabet Ney, stand at the north on either side of the entrance to the central rotunda. Their grouping is significant, for these four pieces provide, both chronologically and thematically, an appropriate introduction to the remaining art within the building.

---

[7] John Adams to Abigail Adams, Apr. 27, 1777, *Adams Family Correspondence*, ed. L[yman] H. Butterfield (4 vols.; Cambridge, Mass.; Belknap Press of Harvard University Press, 1963–1973), II, 224, 225 (quotation). On John Trumbull, see Irma B. Jaffe, *John Trumbull: Patriot-Artist of the American Revolution* (Boston: New York Graphic Society, 1975), and Helen A. Cooper (ed.), *John Trumbull: The Hand and Spirit of a Painter* (New Haven: Yale Univeristy Art Gallery, 1982). For Charles Willson Peale, the essays in Edgar P. Richardson, Brook Hindle, and Lillian B. Miller, *Charles Willson Peale and His World* (New York: Harry N. Abrams, 1982) are informative.

They all deal with figures and events that were instrumental in wresting Texas from Mexico; taken together, they construct an allegorical narrative of the state's eventual domination by Anglo-Saxon men.[8]

Huddle's 1889 portrait of Davy Crockett (fig. 1), for example, is the depiction of an actual historical figure—the Tennessee frontiersman who fought and died at the Alamo—and it certainly utilizes some aspects of the hero's popular image. Huddle, for example, depicts Crockett in the costume for which he was best known. Standing appropriately in the midst of the forest, the frontiersman wears a buckskin suit and leggings and grasps both his proverbial coonskin cap and his famous rifle, "Old Betsy." At the same time, Huddle hardly portrays him as the rough and comic figure of legend; far from being the hero depicted in *Davy Crockett's Almanack*, this Crockett is one of nature's noblemen, an idea Huddle has carefully emphasized on both a narrative and a formal level.[9]

Rather than being involved in some wild escapade, the frontiersman stands still and firm, gazing thoughtfully into the distance. In a formal sense, Huddle has anchored the figure squarely in the center of the canvas by countering the parallel lines of tree, rifle, tunic opening, and right arm with the crossed diagonals of Crockett's pouch strap in one direction and his sheathed knife and raised forearm in the other. The diagonal of the strap also accentuates the turn of Crockett's head. By having the frontiersman look into the distance rather than at the viewer, Huddle emphasizes the timeless nature of his subject, a quality that the lack of any background except the primeval forest also reinforces. No details detract from the noble appearance of the subject. His buckskin is spotless, his hair smoothed back and glistening, and his coonskin cap removed from his head—at least as much to keep him from looking ridiculous, one suspects, as to signify his respectfulness and humility. Finally, without any concrete or unique references to his identity, Crockett becomes an abstraction, a Texan Everyman, embodying virtues of bravery, simplicity, and ease in nature.

---

[8] On the placement of these works, see below and Austin *Daily Statesman*, Feb. 1, 1891.

[9] William Henry Huddle (1847–1892) was born in Virginia and joined his family in Paris, Texas, after the Civil War. He received art training in New York at the National Academy of Design and the Art Student's League during the mid-1870s and later went to Germany, where he studied at the Munich Academy. The majority of the paintings to appear in the Texas Capitol at the turn of the century were Huddle's. For more information on Huddle, see Pauline A. Pinckney, *Painting in Texas: The Nineteenth Century* (Austin: University of Texas Press, 1967), 196–203. For other images of Crockett, see Frederick S. Voss, "Portraying an American Original: The Likenesses of Davy Crockett," *Southwestern Historical Quarterly*, XCI (Apr., 1988), 457–482. An article in the Austin *Daily Statesman*, Feb. 1, 1891, entitled "Superb Pictures," claims that the Huddle painting is based on a photograph of a portrait by Rembrandt Peale, which is currently unlocated.

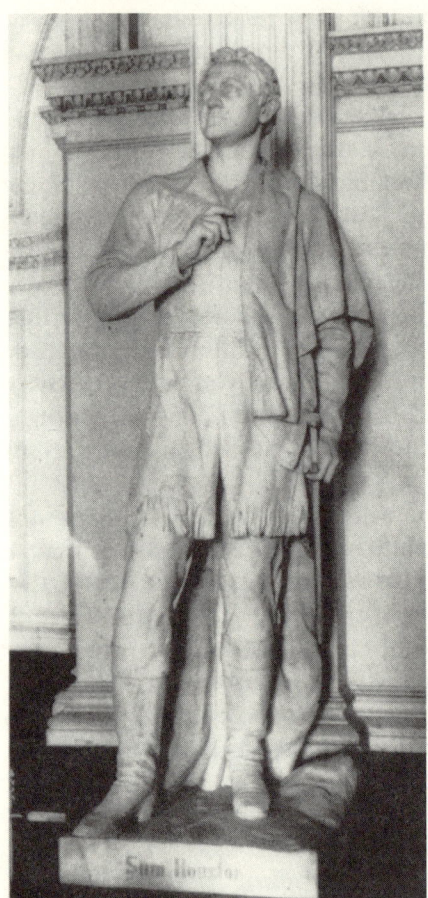

Figure 2. *Sam Houston* by Elisabet Ney, 1902. Marble, 82½ inches. *Courtesy Austin History Center, Austin Public Library.*

Figure 3. *Stephen F. Austin* by Elisabet Ney, 1902. Marble, 76½ inches. *Courtesy Austin History Center, Austin Public Library.*

The statues of Sam Houston (fig. 2) and Stephen F. Austin (fig. 3) that stand at the northern end of the foyer also exemplify those ideals. Originally modeled by Elisabet Ney for exhibition at the 1893 Chicago World's Fair, the two figures represent different aspects of the Texas Everyman. When Ney began working on the statues in the fall of 1892, she wrote descendants of both heroes asking for descriptions, likenesses, and artifacts. After some research, she informed Houston's daughter Margaret H. Williams that she had decided to emphasize "the statesman as well as the soldier" in her father and would model the portrait accordingly. The resulting figure, with its simple lines and balanced pose, is clearly related to other statues of soldier-statesmen from antiquity to the nineteenth century. Its calm repose, purposeful gaze, and erect stance place it within the artistic tradition of figures such as the Louvre's statue of Augustus Caesar or Jean-Antoine Houdon's *George Washington* in the Capitol at Richmond, Virginia. The sword that Houston grasps with his left hand signifies his strength and power as a military leader, while the Mexican blanket drapes over his left shoulder and falls to the ground, giving the appearance of a Roman toga.[10]

Although both Houston and Austin appear in the buckskin that Ney, like Huddle, apparently associated with ideas of natural nobility, the attributes of the Austin statue differentiate it from its companion piece. A tree stump that supports the standing figure signifies Austin's function as settler and civilizer, as do the rifle, powder horn, and map. The Kentucky long rifle that Austin cradles was the premier weapon of the American woodlands and, because of the difficulty associated with its loading, was more useful to settlers than to soldiers. The rifle is at rest in Austin's arms, while the powder horn is laid aside on the tree stump. Rather than a weapon, Austin grasps a scroll, which on a literal level is a map to the territory the empresario would settle. It also resembles a religious, scholarly, or legal document and thus refers specifically to Austin's attempts to bring the Anglo-American legal system to settlers in Mexican Texas, an act that represented to many the struggle of civilization against barbarism.[11]

Like the portrait of Crockett, the statues of Houston and Austin have an obvious allegorical quality, one their positions reinforce. Significantly, when the state commissioned Ney to produce marble versions of the two statues for the Capitol in 1902, a rather heated discussion ensued between the sculptor and then governor Joseph D. Sayers about their proper placement. Sayers apparently wanted the statues on the second floor, but Ney insisted they stand in front of the pilasters on either side of the entrance to the rotunda. Not forgetting her original

---

[10] Elisabet Ney (1833–1907) was born in Munster, Westphalia, educated at the Munich and Berlin Academies of Art, and completed numerous portraits of significant European personalities before immigrating to the United States in 1871. The statues of Houston and Austin were her first major works in Texas, where she lived from 1873 until her death. Draft of letter, Elisabet Ney to Margaret Houston Williams, 1892–1893 notebook, n.p. (quotation) (Harry Ransom Humanities Research Center, Univeristy of Texas at Austin). See also Emily Fourmy Cutrer, *The Art of the Woman: The Life and Work of Elisabet Ney* (Lincoln: University of Nebraska Press, 1988), 126, 132–136, 139–141.

[11] See Cutrer, *Art of the Woman*, 132, 137–143.

Figure 4. The statues of Houston and Austin in place in the south foyer of the Capitol. *Courtesy HABS.*

plan for art in the building, Ney consciously designed the two statues as a pair to be placed exactly as they are now (fig. 4). Just as her two subjects had reciprocal social functions as soldier and settler, statesman and jurist, their artistic forms complement each other. Austin's lowered arms balance Houston's raised right hand, while both turn away from the rotunda in a mirror-image motion. In addition, each figure's attributes appear on the side that leads into the center of the Capitol. Thus, the two statues perform a function analogous to that which the two men served in life. Just as the soldier and the empresario had ushered Anglo-American civilization into Texas, the portraits of Houston and Austin literally show the way to all those who walk into the heart of the Capitol, the state's most important public symbol.[12]

The fourth work in the foyer, Huddle's depiction of *The Surrender of Santa Anna* (fig. 5), is a natural culmination of the narrative that begins with the portrait of Crockett, the man of the woods, on the east, and progresses through Ney's soldier and settler at the north. In a seem-

---

[12] Ney to Ella Dibrell, Oct. 1, 1902 (Elisabet Ney Museum, Austin). The *Sam Houston* and *Stephen F. Austin* that now stand in the State Capitol were cut in marble in 1902 after the original plaster casts, completed in 1893 for the World's Columbian Exposition.

Figure 5. *The Surrender of Santa Anna* by William Henry Huddle, 1890. Oil on canvas, 71 × 113 inches. *Courtesy Archives Division, Texas State Library.*

ingly straightforward manner, it illustrates the event that marked the dawning of Anglo-Texan preeminence in the region. Quite simply, Huddle depicts the meeting of Sam Houston and General Antonio López de Santa Anna on April 22, 1836, the day after the Texans' rout of the Mexican army at San Jacinto. The positions of two foreground figures, Houston's physician on the left and Deaf Smith on the right, direct the viewer's attention to the event taking place in the center of the painting. The wounded Texan general reclines beneath the famous Treaty Oak and with his outstretched arm indicates Santa Anna, who wears the blue-jacketed uniform of a regular soldier. Assembled around the main actors are some thirty Texans who supposedly participated in the surrender at the battleground, as well as Santa Anna's aide, Juan N. Almonte, who appears just behind Houston's arm in a red-breasted uniform. Except for the few figures on the left who threaten and are restrained from violence against Santa Anna, these witnesses appear as stiff, paper-doll figures who have been pasted on the canvas with their heads virtually strung out on a line.

Despite its technical flaws, the painting is culturally significant, and its importance stems in large part from its ritualistic and communal aspect. Indeed, one reason the image seems so stiff is because of its symmetrical composition. Moving in from the outer edges, the rifles of the two Texans guarding the cannon on the right counter the action of the man with upstretched arm on the left; the physician and Deaf Smith balance each other in the foreground; while Santa Anna and Almonte are roughly equidistant from the center. As in a medieval triptych or a Gothic church, such symmetry has a connotative function; it emphasizes the solemnity of the occasion as well as its eternal significance and transforms the painting into a secular version of an altarpiece. At the same time, the witnesses become a congregation, and their participation in Santa Anna's surrender underscores the event's significance for a larger community. They remind the viewer not only that large numbers took part in the events leading up to Texas's independence, but also that the Texan victory at San Jacinto affected a larger group than those immediately present.

The witnesses also turn the painting into a visual history text. In the tradition of Trumbull's *Declaration of Independence*, in which any American schoolchild should be able to recognize at least Thomas Jefferson, Benjamin Franklin, and John Hancock, Huddle's participants are almost all identifiable personalities with individual stories. The figure kneeling between Santa Anna and Almonte, for example, is Moses Austin Bryan, the nephew of Stephen F. Austin, who acted as interpreter for Houston and Santa Anna and later alternated farm life with public and military service in a pattern that was typical of the individuals included in the painting. Anson Jones, who stands just to the left of Treaty Oak wearing an unlikely white shirt, tie, and frock coat, was a physician who served the Republic of Texas as its last president; John Austin Wharton, who appears at Jones's right, a lawyer by training, was related to one of the area's most prominent plantation families, and served in the Texas Congress; and Thomas J. Rusk, another figure in the background, left his law practice in order to join Sam Houston in Washington, D.C., as one of the state's first senators. By incorporating such individuals into the painting, Huddle neatly resolved one of the central paradoxes of art in a democratic republic. By selecting figures who were notable not for their individual accomplishments alone, but also for their records of personal sacrifice to a larger cause, he both immortalized the unique individuals and glorified their communal endeavor.

He also created a canvas that looks forward in time from the event represented. While *The Surrender of Santa Anna* culminates the narrative represented in the art of the front foyer, it also deals with assumptions inherent in the art of the rotunda, paintings that depict significant figures in post–San Jacinto Texas. If Huddle's canvas is a primer in republican virtue, the pictures that adorn the walls of the rotunda form an encyclopedia. Forty-seven paintings, portraits of every Texas president and governor, ring the rotunda from the first floor to the fourth. As a series devoted to significant public figures, these paintings are not a unique concept. They are undoubtedly related to two similar projects, *The Great Men of France* series in the Louvre, initiated in 1776 by the Count d'Angiviller, and National Statuary Hall in Washington, D.C., which was established to fill the former House chamber by an act of Congress in 1864. Because every elected governor is represented, the series avoids the problem of selection inherent in the other two projects, while its placement in the heart of the building gives it even greater didactic significance than the others. As Elisabet Ney no doubt recognized when she suggested busts in the rotunda, the placement of the portraits is similar to that of the Roman gods who circle the interior of the Pantheon. Thus, the subjects are modern secular equivalents of the ancient deities and embody the official values of the state that commissioned and placed their portraits, ideas that the first paintings in the series best exemplify.

In 1888 the Twentieth Legislature appropriated ten thousand dollars to purchase "statuary and portraits for the rotunda." Most of that sum went to the painter William Henry Huddle, who for several years had been compiling his own gallery of Texas presidents and governors. Working from old engravings and photographs, Huddle had completed twenty portraits that the state bought for seven thousand dollars. As paintings, these works seem rather unremarkable at first, in part because they are so similar. Huddle presents each of the individuals in an identical format. The portraits are all bust-length with dark-toned backgrounds, and each subject wears a dark coat, white shirt, and dark tie. Not even Sam Houston, who was known for his colorful clothing, breaks the mold. Although the poses vary slightly, with some of the presidents and governors turning one way or another while others look straight ahead, their expressions are similarly tight-lipped and grave.[13]

This manner of presentation, of course, emphasizes the formal solemnity of the portraits; because of their background, dress, and expression, the attentive viewer knows these are persons whom one must take seriously. At the same time, the uniformity of format enhances their differences. As in *The Surrender of Santa Anna,* Huddle has carefully worked out each individual's likeness. In some portraits, such as

---

[13] H. P. N. Gammel (comp.), *The Laws of Texas, 1822–1897* . . . (10 vols.; Austin: Gammel Book Co., 1898), IX, 1,016. Pinckney, *Painting in Texas,* 201, incorrectly cites the source as *Journal of the Senate, Twentieth Legislature, Called Session, (1888),* 18 ($10,000 appropriation for presidents and governors of Texas).

Figure 6. *Edmund J. Davis* by
William Henry Huddle, 1880.
Oil on canvas, 30 × 25 inches.
*Courtesy Archives Division, Texas
State Library.*

those of J. Pinckney Henderson and Pendleton Murrah, the images are
wooden and unnatural, while in others, such as those of Edmund J.
Davis and John Ireland (fig. 6), they are compellingly human and real.
Despite the variation in quality, however, each portrait, like each subject, is unique.

What Huddle has done with these paintings is similar to what he
worked out in *The Surrender*. He has resolved that tension within democratic culture between the emphasis on individualism and the needs of
the community. By stressing the individual's likeness in these portraits,
he has provided real models for emulation—unique personalities one
may point to, learn about, and then aspire to resemble. Yet, by utilizing
a standard format, he has also emphasized their communal function.
Their equality, in other words, balances their uniqueness and ensures
that the cult of a single individual does not outweigh the significance of
his community service. The very somber, formal style of the portraits is
therefore appropriate, for the paintings are not intended to excite
emotion but to inspire thought. For that reason as well, the bust format
is logical. It directs the viewer's attention toward the subject's face and
emphasizes his powers of reason and contemplation, attributes highly
valued in republican ideology as significant for every citizen, but particularly for public officials.

The formal, iconlike quality of the rotunda portraits characterizes
much of the remaining art within the Capitol. Except for a handful of

Figure 7. *The Settlement of Austin's Colony* by Henry McArdle, 1875. Oil on canvas, 83 × 60 inches. *Courtesy Archives Division, Texas State Library.*

paintings in various offices and the gallery of justices on the third floor, most of the portraits may be found in the House and Senate chambers. In each case, pictures commemorating important figures line the sides of the room, culminating at the front in symmetrical arrangements that underscore their ceremonial aspect. Like those under the dome, these portraits, even when they depict full figures, are straightforward works whose main distinguishing feature is their subjects' likeness.

This emphasis on portraiture at least partially informs the three history paintings that appear in the legislative chambers, *The Settlement of Austin's Colony* in the House, and *Dawn at the Alamo* and *The Battle of San Jacinto* in the Senate, all by the nineteenth-century artist Henry A. McArdle. As he would for the latter two canvases, McArdle provided a key to reading *Austin's Colony* (fig. 7), the first of the paintings to be completed. Describing this painting to James T. DeShields of San Antonio, an early Texas art patron and historian, he wrote that the work depicted Stephen F. Austin and several other prominent figures in his colony as news of an Indian raid interrupts them in their task of issuing land. McArdle also carefully identified each of the participants in the incident, from Baron de Bastrop, the Mexican land commissioner, barely visible on the left, to Horatio Chriesman, a surveyor drawing a map on the floor to the right, to Ran Foster, a hunter, and Samuel May Williams, the colonial secretary, above.

Despite its specificity, McArdle was, nevertheles, well aware of the allegorical significance of the scene, and particularly of Austin's function in it. He described the historical figure as "reading from a book marked 'Laws of Mexico'" and wearing a sword "illustrative of his authority as Judge and commander of the Colonial troops." These attributes, along with the rifle for which he reaches, were "suggestive," McArdle wrote, "of the Empressario's [*sic*] many duties and fearful trials of Colonization." They also indicate his status as the carrier of civilization into the wilderness. The cabins burning in the background have been set afire by "savages," but Austin, whose portrait not only commands the attention of the other figures in the painting but also dominates the canvas, betrays no unseemly anxiety or fright. Rather, he appears both calm and resolute as he grasps his rifle in a motion reminiscent of such rallying gestures as Liberty's, to cite one example, as she carries the French flag in Eugène Delacroix's *Liberty Leading the People*.[14]

Although such a comparison may seem ludicrous, given the vastly different style and the obvious technical inferiority of McArdle's canvas to the Frenchman's, it may nevertheless be instructive. Like Delacroix's *Liberty,* most of McArdle's work has an obvious allegorical and patriotic element, yet McArdle liked to cast himself in the mold of painter-historian. Indeed, he spent decades researching the scenes he depicted in *Dawn at the Alamo* and *The Battle of San Jacinto.* He tracked historical accounts of the two battles, located witnesses and survivors, and collected artifacts of clothing and weapons. He even went so far as to gather all his notes and correspondence in two enormous volumes in order to vouch for the accuracy of his paintings to later generations. As he wrote on one occasion: "My positions and views in art, in brief, may be summed up as follows: No color, however magnificent, no line, however subtle, can make a work of art. Without expression, truth, and a story told, the canvas had better been left untouched." Yet despite all his emphasis on historical accuracy, McArdle's "truth" transcended fact and his stories had a moral. A comparison between McArdle's depic-

---

[14] Henry A. McArdle to James T. DeShields, Mar. 13, 1906 (quotation) (Daughters of the Republic of Texas Library at the Alamo, San Antonio), cited in Pinckney, *Painting in Texas,* 195. The portion of this letter to DeShields explicating McArdle's painting is also reproduced on a label beneath the painting in the House chamber.

Henry Arthur McArdle (1836–1907) was born in Northern Ireland and immigrated to Baltimore, Maryland, in 1850. According to Pinckney, he trained at the Maryland Institute for the Promotion of the Mechanic Arts, served as a draftsman in the Confederate navy, and moved to Independence, Texas, in 1867–1868, where he taught art at Baylor Female College for more than two decades. See Pinckney, *Painting in Texas,* 190–195.

Figure 8. *The Battle of the Alamo* by Theodore Gentilz, c. 1885. Oil on canvas, original destroyed. *Courtesy Barker Texas History Center, University of Texas at Austin.*

tion of the Alamo with that by another artist, Theodore Gentilz, completed nearly fifty years before, demonstrates the subjective use to which the Irishman put his research.[15]

Gentilz was a Frenchman who emigrated to Texas in 1844 with Henri Castro as part of that entrepreneur's attempt to plant a French colony in Texas in an area just west of San Antonio. Trained at L'Ecole Impériale des Mathématiques et de Dessin in Paris, Gentilz had joined the expedition as an engineer and surveyor. The architecture and history of the missions in San Antonio, however, appealed to his aesthetic sense, and he soon abandoned his position in Castroville to take up an artist's career. One of the first subjects he undertook in Texas was a depiction of the battle of the Alamo (fig. 8), an event that was still fresh in the minds of many in San Antonio. Apparently Gentilz interviewed a number of witnesses and spent a great deal of time examining and sketching the mission's grounds. His technical training undoubtedly influenced the use to which he put such information. Topography, architecture, and troop formation receive equal emphasis in his depiction of the event. Seen at a distance and from above, the mission virtually melts into the landscape, and the Mexican troops seem mere stick figures as

---

[15] See "H. A. McArdle's Companion to the Battle Paintings, Historical Documents, Vol. I—Dawn at the Alamo"; and "H. A. McArdle's Companion to the Battle Paintings, Historical Documents, Vol. II—The Battle at San Jacinto," Manuscript Collection (Archives Division, Texas State Library, Austin). These two leather-bound volumes contain McArdle's notes, correspondence, and descriptions of the two paintings. For quotation, see Vol. I, 8.

they advance toward the Alamo on the morning of the battle. The distancing lends an eerie quiet and stillness to the scene, a calm before the storm, while the bird's-eye view shows none of the death and destruction one might naturally expect.[16]

Gentilz's dispassion thus contrasts sharply with the more predictable violence in McArdle's *Dawn at the Alamo* (fig. 9), completed in 1905, nearly sixty years later. At first glance, the Irishman's painting seems to replicate the kind of confusion and disorder normally associated with battle. McArdle literally filled the canvas with isolated depictions of struggle and hand-to-hand combat. In the lower left, a figure whom McArdle identified as Major Robert Evans fires the Texans' last magazine, while a wraithlike Jim Bowie rises from his deathbed to fend off the Mexicans. Davy Crockett battles opponents to their left, while William B. Travis, on the barracks above him, fires his pistol at an enemy soldier. Bodies litter the floor of the compound, while Mexicans breach the walls in great numbers. At the same time, McArdle's abrupt cropping at the bottom and sides pulls the viewer into the melee; the edge of the canvas chops off figures and thus suggests a continuity between the painting and the world outside it.

The painting is hardly a random collection of unconnected events, however, for McArdle has carefully manipulated the image in order to present his own version of the incident. Despite his research and claims of veracity, the artist has given here neither a factual nor an objective view of the battle at the Alamo. As several historians have pointed out, McArdle's placement of Crockett, Travis, and Bowie is in error. Travis died at the beginning of the battle rather than toward the end, as the painting suggests, and Crockett was on the other side of the mission from his commander instead of just below. Whether McArdle knew this or not, he was at least partially aware of other inaccuracies. In his gloss of the painting, for example, the artist admitted that Jim Bowie was "idealized"—that he was not in the middle of the fight as depicted, but was dying in his bed in the convent. For McArdle, the "idealized" version of Bowie, "flourishing for the last time the terrible knife to which he gave his name," was somehow more true to the spirit of the event than a factual depiction would have been. Undoubtedly his inclusion of other individuals who had not been on the scene stemmed from the same sentiment.[17]

---

[16] For information on Gentilz, see Pinckney, *Painting in Texas*, 99–118, and Dorothy Steinbomer Kendall and Carmen Perry, *Gentilz: Artist of the Old Southwest* (Austin: University of Texas Press, 1974).

[17] Sam DeShong Ratcliffe, "Texas History Painting: An Iconographic Study" (Ph.D. diss., University of Texas at Austin, 1985), 62; "Companion to the Battle Paintings . . . Vol. I," 10 (quotations).

Figure 9. *Dawn of the Alamo* by Henry McArdle, 1905. Oil on canvas, 83 × 143 feet. *Courtesy Archives Division, Texas State Library.*

By bringing the Alamo's best-known heroes together, it is significant to note, McArdle was only doing on canvas what the battle's chroniclers have done in other media. Most accounts of the Alamo, from print to film, have dealt with the Texans not only as a group, but also as specific individuals. Anyone who has read a book or seen a movie about the battle undoubtedly knows that James Bowie, Davy Crockett, and William Barrett Travis, for example, played some significant role in the event, and could probably recount something of each hero's background. Unlike most single paintings, however, film and written accounts have a narrative structure with an unfolding sequence of events. McArdle, in contrast, had to present everyone simultaneously. Undoubtedly he did so because he realized that what he was dealing with was not a simple image but a story—or more explicitly, what anthropologists, psychoanalysts, or literary critics would call myth.

A myth, as Ruth F. Benedict and Mircea Eliade, for example, have defined it, is not a superstitious tale or something that is untrue. It is instead a culture's communal explanation or justification of what it is and how it came to be. A "novelistic tale," as Benedict has called it, a myth is a narrative, or sequence of events, with a complex structure of symbols and figures. These figures are significant because they embody and define a people's history and provide rules and models for behavior in much the way that Bowie, Crockett, and Travis inform traditional accounts of the Alamo.[18]

Indeed, given McArdle's notion of painting as story, he had to include all three figures in his canvas, for each represents an essential element in the battle's narrative. Travis, the South Carolina–born lawyer, embodies, on one hand, the virtues of the aristocratic South, a distinction not lost on McArdle. He appears in *Dawn at the Alamo,* as he undoubtedly did at the battle, in the uniform befitting his social and military rank, and he strides across the barracks roof above the general melee and apart from the volunteers. Nevertheless, numerous formal devices, such as the Mexicans' bayonets, as well as the grotesque distortions of his figure, draw the viewer's eye to the Alamo's commander, emphasizing his significance and his individual acts of bravery and also connecting him to the figures on the ground. Bowie and Crockett, on the other hand, embody a somewhat different plot line. Born in Tennessee, both were archetypal frontiersmen, untutored in the social graces but naturally aware of the virtues of liberty and democracy. Sig-

---

[18] Mircea Eliade, *Myth and Reality,* trans. Willard R. Trask (New York: Harper & Row, 1963), 8; Ruth Benedict, "Myth," in Edwin R. A. Seligman (ed.), *Encyclopedia of the Social Sciences* (12 vols.; New York: Macmillan, 1930), XI, 178 (quotation), 179–181.

Figure 10. Detail of *Dawn of the Alamo.*

nificantly, McArdle shows them in the thick of things wearing the every-day dress of volunteers, those who presumably fight not because they have to, but because they believe in the cause.

These three, along with the handful of other Texans whom McArdle specifically portrays, unite in the face of a common enemy. In fact, the virtues, or code of behavior, they represent find their most telling expression in the contrast between the painter's heroes and the Mexicans. In each of the major conflicts in the canvas, those that involve Evans and Bowie on the left, Crockett on the right, Travis above, and an un-identified Texan on the structure in the center, the Anglo-Americans strike heroic poses. The Mexicans, however, graphically illustrate John Adams's injunction that art should perpetuate "to posterity the horrid deeds of our enemies." Time and again they seem to take unfair advantage of the defenders and, in comparison, appear cowardly or animal-like. One, for example, stands frozen with a ferocious leer upon his face, poised to bayonet Travis in the back. A similar expression marks the face of the Mexican soldier at whom Bowie lunges.

Perhaps the most striking contrast is between Davy Crockett and the Mexican soldier whose rifle he pushes aside (fig. 10). By placing the two figures virtually face to face, McArdle revealed his Manichean vision of the combatants. Crockett and the Mexican are not merely two men;

they are two races that represent opposing forces in the painter's mind. Significantly, the light that falls on the Texan emphasizes his whiteness; his shirt sleeve and chest virtually glow, while his hair, which in reality was black, here appears almost sandy. With his arm outstretched like one of Jacques Louis David's Horatii brothers, he appears strong, fearless, and noble. In comparison, the Mexican is evil, and the light that also falls upon him only accentuates his darkness. Although he is not actually crouching, he appears at least to crumple under Crockett's arm, and his face is almost apelike in its ferociousness and stupidity. Like many of his fellow Anglo-Americans, McArdle obviously subscribed to views that not only assumed the racial and cultural inferiority of those with dark skins but also associated moral depravity with persons of mixed breeding, such as Crockett's opponent appears to be.[19]

As a result, McArdle's painting is a visual morality play dealing with the opposites of light and dark, good and evil—and, like most myths, it has a religious significance that the formal organization of the canvas further exemplifies. Indeed, the confusion in McArdle's painting is more apparent than real. Just as the individual Texans are ultimately united by their overarching goal or ideal, the isolated incidents in the painting are connected in a larger scheme. Dominating the underlying structure of the composition is a central triangle with Evans and Crockett marking the bottom points and the scarlet flag at the center of the canvas, its apex. That flag, with its location and brilliant color, is one of the numerous devices that McArdle used to call the viewer's attention to the structure in the center mid-ground (fig. 11). McArdle undoubtedly exaggerated the proportions of this structure—a platform the Texans had built so that a cannon might be fired over the walls—in order to emphasize its symbolic importance. The platform becomes a sacrificial altar, and the story being acted out upon it has the same crucial significance to the Texas myth that the cross has to Christianity.[20]

The figures who struggle atop the platform are, in effect, allegorized versions of the individuals who fight to either side and below. As in the rest of the painting, the Mexicans physically overwhelm the Texans, but their victory, as the episode attests, is ultimately meaningless. Significantly, the flag that descends in a classic gesture of defeat is not, as

---

[19] For a discussion of these views, see Arnoldo De León, *They Called Them Greasers: Anglo Attitudes toward Mexicans in Texas, 1821–1900* (Austin: University of Texas Press, 1983), especially ch. 2 and 8.

[20] McArdle's sketches of this structure in "Companion to the Battle Paintings . . . Vol. I" seem to indicate the importance that he attached to it. The volume also contains a letter to McArdle from Captain Rufus M. Potter, Oct. 3, 1874, indicating that he understood the structure to have an allegorical significance.

Figure 11. Detail of *Dawn of the Alamo.*

one might expect, that of the Texans. Rather, it is the "blood-red" banner, as McArdle called it, of "no quarter" that a Mexican soldier drops as he topples during his ascent. For the Texans, this flag represented one of the most abhorrent aspects of the Alamo—the refusal of the Mexican leader Santa Anna to take prisoners; and the martyrdom of every Alamo defender has, of course, lent mythic proportions to the struggle. More than one commentator, including McArdle, has likened the battle to that at Thermopylae, where more than five hundred Spartan warriors died, defending a strategic pass against an invading Persian army. As at Thermopylae, moreover, the actions of the victor spurred the losing side to vengeance. Thus the Mexicans, McArdle apparently reasoned, brought about their own downfall: in *Dawn at the Alamo,* the officer who carries the flag is accidentally shot by another Mexican officer on the gun platform.[21]

By calling the viewer's attention to the contrasting clouds above and below, the blood-red banner also literally points to what is to come. While the sky above the Alamo is a dark and blood-red reflection of the action beneath, "the blaze of orange and gold" in the lower distance signals the sunrise. Ever the allegorist, McArdle pointed out both in his notes and on the picture frame that the morning had symbolic significance. The dawn of the new day was also, as he emphasized, "*the dawn of liberty to Texas.*" Fittingly, a single silver star shines faintly in the heavens above, a star that McArdle identified as the Lone Star of Texas.[22]

The Battle of San Jacinto, which hangs to the right of *Dawn at the Alamo* (fig. 12) in the Senate, brings McArdle's narrative to its conclusion. A similarly huge canvas, it depicts what the painter saw as the natural result of the Mexican actions at the earlier battle. Sam Houston, his officers, and troops storm the enemy's breastworks to apply what McArdle termed "Retributive Justice." Scores of Mexicans lie dead on the field, while hundreds of others fight or flee from the Texans' assault. Like its companion piece, the work is intricately detailed; even in five ledger-size sheets, McArdle was unable to provide what he believed to be an adequate written description. Of the hundreds of figures on the canvas, more than fifty are portraits that he carefully identified in the accompanying key. In contrast to *Dawn at the Alamo,* however, at least a few are sympathetic portrayals of Mexicans. In his notes, McArdle described the enemy troops in the foreground and left of center as "bravely holding on to the breastwork, led by the heroic [General Manuel Fer-

---

[21] McArdle, "Brief Description or Reading of the Painting," in "Companion to Battle Paintings . . . Vol. I," 10.

[22] Ibid.

Figure 12. *The Battle of San Jacinto* by Henry McArdle, 1898. Oil on canvas, 92 × 167 feet. *Courtesy Archives Division, Texas State Library.*

nandez] Castrillon" and referred to several other officers as "gallant Mexicans." These men stood their ground, while Santa Anna, for whom McArdle and most Texas partisans held a particular scorn, fled. The Napoleon of the West, in fact, behaved so infamously that the artist depicts him riding off on his horse between two mules who buck and balk because, as McArdle wrote, even they "have lost respect for him."[23]

Despite his antiquarian's love of anecdote, McArdle realized truth might be lost in too "slavish" a transcription of the battle's conduct. Thus, as in *Dawn at the Alamo,* he uses the sky and the time of day to unify his "multitude of figures" and "wealth of episode" and to carry the painting's transcendent meaning. The "dark, inauspicious and threatening clouds," he wrote, "overspread the heavens" and signify the "suffering, danger and death under which Texas had struggled." Nevertheless, the "rays of the setting sun break through the gloom" and indicate that "light and freedom and liberty" result from the scene below. *San Jacinto,* in other words, brings to fruition the liberty presaged by *Dawn at the Alamo,* and in its strong movement to the right suggests at the same time that the story begun in the first canvas continues into the future.[24]

The theme of these paintings is also conveyed by the monuments standing on the Capitol grounds. Although they are of a different genre and are simple and abstract in comparison to McArdle's grandiose visions of bravery and battle, these works do nothing to contradict the cultural biases of the art inside the Capitol. Indeed, they also contribute to the construction of a Texas story, or mythology, as the first work to appear on the grounds, the *Monument to the Heroes of the Alamo,* completed in 1891, illustrates (fig. 13).[25]

Commissioned by the Twenty-first Legislature in 1889 to replace a small memorial that had been destroyed in the 1881 Capitol fire, the memorial is a predominantly architectural work designed and constructed by a monument firm in Kentucky. Built of Texas granite, it is essentially a cupola formed by four arches surmounting a square base. Emblems of battle and death appear in low relief on the tympana within the arches, names of those who fought at the Alamo are carved on the inner face of the supporting pillars, and a statue of a soldier carrying his long rifle rises from the structure's apex.[26]

---

[23] McArdle, "Brief Description or Reading of the Painting," in "Companion to Battle Paintings . . . Vol. II," 25–29.

[24] Ibid., 25 (1st and 2nd quotations), 26–28, 29 (3rd–8th quotations).

[25] Ibid.

[26] Austin *Daily Statesman,* Jan. 16, 1891.

Figure 13. Monument to the heroes of the Alamo on the grounds of the Capitol. *Courtesy Archives Division, Texas State Library.*

When an Austin *Statesman* reporter covered the monument's completion for the newspaper, vocabulary failed him. He was able to explain
the engineering methods used in the monument's construction and to
describe, if not analyze, its appearance. But the best aesthetic assess-
ment he could muster was that "it is safe to say that there now exists no
handsomer or more appropriate monument than this." Intuitively,
however, he understood the work's symbolic significance, particularly
as it was represented in the eight-foot statue that crowns the structure.
An undistinguished piece that resembles countless other figures that
appear on monuments from the period, the statue's lack of distinction
is also, as the reporter realized, its most noteworthy aspect. Rather than
any specific individual, the statue represents, he wrote, "the hardy, stalwart son of Texas." He is the archetypal Texan, significantly depicted as
a protector rather than as an aggressor, and he appears, in the reporter's words, as he "stepped from between the handles of the plow to
pick up his long rifle and set his face against the swa[r]ming hosts who
came from Mexico to sweep freedom forever from his fireside." Thus,
as in McArdle's depiction of the battles at the Alamo and at San Jacinto,
little sense of irony or complexity informs either the monument or the
reporter's explication of it. As they both imply, the situation was quite
simple: the Anglo-Texan who fought at the Alamo was a brave individual defending his peaceful homestead against the uncivilized and mur-
derous hordes.[27]

This same theme—Texan soldiers as righteous and noble defenders—reappears in works dedicated to the other major event commemorated at the Capitol, the American Civil War. As historian Charles R.
Wilson has shown, by 1880 a kind of civil religion had developed in the
American South that both justified and reconciled Confederate defeat.
Though northern victory had crushed the southerners' bid for a separate political status, Wilson argues that "the dream of a separate Southern identity did not die in 1865." Indeed, many post–Civil War leaders
attempted to insure that the southern cause, with its image of a chosen
people designated to carry out God's plan on earth, was not entirely
lost. Combining Christian rhetoric, ritual, and symbols with the rhetoric and imagery of the Confederacy, these southerners forged a link
between the region's religion and its history in order to create a "co-
hesive Southern people" with a separate cultural identity."[28]

---

[27] Austin *Daily Statesman*, Apr. 26, 1891.
[28] Charles Reagan Wilson, *Baptized in Blood: The Religion of the Lost Cause, 1865–1920* (Athens:
University of Georgia Press, 1980), 1.

One of the major icons of this civil religion was the Confederate monument. By 1914 more than a thousand dotted the southern landscape. While Civil War memorials became virtually ubiquitous on East Texas courthouse lawns in the decades around the turn of the century, several groups began efforts to construct major monuments on the Texas Capitol grounds. In 1895, for example, the United Confederate Camps of Texas created a committee of distinguished members to solicit public contributions for a memorial at the Capitol dedicated "to the memory of all the Confederate dead, without distinction as to rank or place of enlistment." Virtually alone among the southern states, the public announcement claimed, "Texas has within her borders a population coming from every other Southern state," and this unique situation imposed "a special duty upon us of caring for the memory of all of the heroes of the 'Lost Cause.'" Few apparently argued publicly with the notion, and in 1895 the Twenty-fourth Legislature authorized the Confederate veterans to construct their memorial on the Capitol grounds' most prominent location, at the head of Congress Avenue, just before the front gates.[29]

Whether from lack of sophistication or lack of funds, or most probably a combination of the two, the group charged with making arrangements for the memorial did not announce a design competition. Instead, the committee—composed of lawyers, businessmen, and wealthy farmers—came up with a proposal itself, one that it believed met its announced requirement that the work be of "first-class artistic conception and execution."[30] The design, similar to that for the Alamo monument, called for a combination of architecture, bas-relief sculpture, and statuary. In contrast to the earlier work, however, the allegory in this memorial was hardly simple or subtle. Indeed, the committee worked out plans for sculptural groups that included so much detail that even Henry McArdle would have been put to shame.

According to its published plan, the Confederate monument would be composed of a large granite base with a smaller granite pedestal arising from the center. On each corner of the base, the plan called for a sculptural group illustrating destruction and death. On one corner of the base would be a tribute to Confederate infantry regiments—a falling standard-bearer being relieved of his task by a comrade reaching over his nearly lifeless body; at a second, a wounded trooper leaning against his horse would represent the cavalry. The third corner, while

[29] "The Monumental Spirit of the South," *Confederate Veteran*, XXII (Aug., 1914), 344, cited in Wilson, *Baptized in Blood*, 29; Austin *Daily Statesman*, Oct. 13, 1895 (quotations).

[30] Austin *Daily Statesman*, Jan. 12, 1897.

less explicitly worked out than the previous two, would commemorate southern artillery by depicting a "broken [gun] carriage, broken wheel, a wounded soldier, leaning comrade with bandage or otherwise." Finally, the fourth corner was to honor the "faithful servant" by depicting a "Negro bareheaded, excited expression in face, etc." in the act of "leading, supporting, or more or less carrying a wounded soldier from the field." Only the committee's prescription for the top group could surpass the clichéd melodrama of these assemblages. On the central pedestal, a soldier representing the Lost Cause would be seen returning home, carrying a staff instead of a gun and revealing an empty sleeve. His face, at the same time sad and "determined," would look into the distance while a kneeling woman, with an expression of "regret and joy," would clutch her hero's hand and knees. Fortunately, though the committee believed such a monument would "be an ornament alike to the capitol and the city," many others thought otherwise, and public debate about its appropriateness appeared in the Austin newspaper for several months. In perhaps the most stinging criticism of the plan, one Austin citizen declared that it was such a monstrosity that, if it were erected as planned, it would "scare imaginative children into fits and . . . drive their elders to suicide or emigration."[31]

The monument undoubtedly offended public taste because it violated what had become traditional form for Civil War memorials. The overwhelming majority of Confederate monuments depicted not scenes of death and destruction, such as the Texas committee plan called for, but a single soldier standing with his rifle at the top of a granite pedestal. This anonymous figure represented not only his own fate, but also that of his fellow soldiers in a manner similar to that of the figure atop the Alamo monument; his erect stance and the separation from onlookers created by his pedestal gave him an air of dignity and respect. It also mirrored the depictions of the few individuals who appeared in Confederate monuments, soldiers such as Robert E. Lee, J. E. B. Stuart, and Thomas J. ("Stonewall") Jackson, who had achieved virtual sainthood in the civil religion of the post–Civil War South and whose solemn and dignified images provided models for its culture.[32]

Thus when the Texas committee members eventually yielded to public demand, they specified a simplified and more conventional memorial (fig. 14). Retaining the original configurations and large size,

---

[31] Austin *Daily Statesman*, Jan. 12, 17 (8th quotation), 30 (1st–7th quotations), 1897.

[32] See Ralph W. Widener, Jr., *Confederate Monuments: Enduring Symbols of the South and the War between the States* (n.p.: Ralph W. Widener, Jr., 1982), for illustrations of most, if not all, of the Confederate monuments.

Figure 14. Confederate monument on the grounds of the Capitol. *Courtesy State Archives, Texas State Library.*

they deleted the melodramatic sculptural groups and substituted four, if not victorious at least undefeated, figures representing the different branches of the Confederate service—the infantry, the artillery, the cavalry, and the navy—at each corner of the base, and a nine-foot statue of Jefferson Davis for the top. Although, as president of the Confederacy, Davis was an appropriate figure for a monument dedicated to soldiers from all the southern states, his placement on the pedestal had even greater significance. Because he was imprisoned and

placed in irons at the end of the war, Davis had transcended his political importance to become an emblem of martyrdom, one who was
frequently compared to Christ by late nineteenth-century southern
preachers and orators. Thus, in its final form, the Confederate monument conformed more closely to the image that the most powerful
Texas citizens had formed of themselves, and by which they apparently
wished later generations to remember them. Rather than death and
defeat, the memorial suggests courage, fortitude, and transcendence.
So does another important work of public sculpture on the Capitol
grounds, the Terry's Texas Rangers monument (fig. 15).[33]

An equestrian statue, the work is one of the first of that genre to
commemorate the Civil War in the South. While historically such sculpture had celebrated specific individuals—Marcus Aurelius or Frederick
the Great, to name two European examples—men whose military prow-
ess matched their abilities as heads of victorious states, this memorial
seems to turn convention on its head: it depicts an anonymous cav-
alryman from the war's losing side. Nevertheless, those involved in the
monument's conception, design, and placement undoubtedly did not
intend to make an ironic comment. To them, Terry's Rangers epito-
mized Texas's contribution to the southern cause, and an equestrian
statue was the group's most fitting tribute.

Organized in 1861 by wealthy South Texas planter Benjamin Franklin Terry, at the request of the Confederate War Department, the cavalry regiment did include, as one of its members admitted, "a good
many rowdys [*sic*]." It also drew volunteers from some of the region's
most important families. College graduates, professional men, mer-
chants, stockmen, and planters, these young men nevertheless gave evidence of their frontier upbringing. They brought with them their own
supplies, including shotguns and pistols, which one recruit commented
they wore "as regularly as clothes," and military order and rank counted
for little among them. As another of their number, Private L. B. Giles
of Company "D" admitted: "From the standpoint of the martinet our
organization could scarcely be called a regiment. If there was ever any
serious attempt to discipline it the effort was soon abandoned. Volunteers we began, volunteers we remained to the end." In the Terry
Rangers, frontier democracy reigned. The regiment elected only such
officers as were necessary; generally, as one of the group later commented, "rank was not considered and when tendered, refused."[34]

---

[33] See Wilson, *Baptized in Blood*, 50–51, for a discussion of Davis as a southern martyr.

[34] See Thomas W. Cutrer, "Introduction," *A Terry Texas Ranger: The Life Record of H. W. Graber* (Austin: State House Books, 1987), ii–iii, iv (1st and 3rd quotations), v (2nd and 4th quotations).

Figure 15. Terry's Texas Rangers monument on the grounds of the Capitol. *Courtesy Austin History Center, Austin Public Library.*

Instead, the most important thing to these volunteers was the ability to ride a horse. One member of Terry's regiment, John Wesley Rabb, wrote home to his mother, "I wood [*sic*] rather be a corporal in Company 'F' of the Texas Rangers than to be a first Lieu in a flat foot company," and apparently he was not alone. During the Civil War recruiters found it difficult to raise infantry in the state because, as one commentator observed, "no Texan walks a yard if he can help it." Talent rather than laziness, however, informed the volunteers' choice of service. In Texas, frontier conditions mixed necessity with the southern chivalric tradition to produce what wartime governor Edward Clark termed "peerless" horsemen, men whose abilities neatly meshed with, and then gave an egalitarian twist to, their culture's ideas about what was noble and dashing in warfare.[35]

The legacy of the original Texas Rangers, to whom they were related only in name, also motivated the regiment. As another of Terry's men, Henry W. Graber, explained, "We started out with the name of 'Texas Rangers,' with a reputation we had never earned but were called on to sustain." By the end of the Civil War, in fact, the legendary status of Terry's group rivaled that of the original Rangers. From Woodsonville, Kentucky, where it first saw action in 1862, to Shiloh, Chickamauga, and Atlanta, the group participated in more than a thousand conflicts and was victorious in over two hundred battles. The soldiers' ability elicited praise from their first commander, Albert Sidney Johnston, who told them, "With a little more drill, you are the equals of the Old Guard of Napoleon," as well as commendations from their final commander, General Joseph Wheeler. "During a four year's [*sic*] struggle for liberty," he said at their disbandment, "you have exhibited courage, fortitude, and devotion."[36]

Thus the Ranger veterans who raised the money, conducted the competition, and finalized plans for the memorial probably never questioned the appropriateness of their equestrian monument. Indeed, to them the Terry's Texas Rangers were not only democratic horsemen, they were also victors. On a literal level—to reverse the emphasis in an old aphorism—they may have lost the war, but they did win their battles. On another level, physical defeat was insignificant; what mattered was spiritual victory, transcendence, or how one had played the game.

Accordingly, at the dedication of the monument in 1907, the keynote speaker followed the pattern set at hundreds of such ritualized events throughout the South. He glossed over the fact that the South had lost the Civil War and dwelt instead on the virtues of Confederate leaders and their men. Robert E. Lee, "the patriotic citizen, the Christian soldier, the great military genius," he claimed, would one day be rightfully

[35] J. W. Rabb to Mary Rabb, June 29, 1862, in Thomas W. Cutrer (ed.), "'We Are Stern and Resolved': The Civil War Letters of John Wesley Rabb, Terry's Texas Rangers," *Southwestern Historical Quarterly*, XCI (Oct., 1987), 202 (1st and 3rd quotations); Walter Lord (ed.), *The Fremantle Diary* . . . (Boston: Little, Brown & Co., 1954), 58 (2nd quotation), cited in Cutrer (ed.), "'We Are Stern and Resolved,'" 202 n.

[36] Cited in Cutrer's introduction to *A Terry Texas Ranger*, iv (1st and 2nd quotations), xxv (3rd quotation).

acknowledged as surpassing "the great military captains of all ages—the Alexanders, the Hannibals, and the Caesars. . . ." He noted that, just a few weeks before, southerners had unveiled a monument "in commemoration of the patriotism, the purity of character and the great statesmanship" of Jefferson Davis. Terry's Rangers, he implied to the large crowd, were of the same caliber: "The record made by . . . that gallant band of Texans—forms one of the bright pages in the history of the Civil War, and deserves to be exemplified in this enduring monument," one intended to "commemorate for all time the patriotism that prompted their enlistment, the hardships they endured, their courage in battle, the death of those who did not survive and the resignation and splendid citizenship of those who returned to their homes. . . ."[37]

Yet if the Rangers were southerners, they were also Texans. Albert Sidney Johnston, one of their band remembered, had found them "a fearless and enthusiastic people, proud of their Texas history," and knew they "would endeavor to emulate the example of the heroes of the Alamo, Goliad and San Jacinto." The orator at the dedication likewise saw the connection between the heroes of the Texas Revolution and those of the Civil War: in his closing remarks he prophesied that, "like the memory of the martyrs of the Alamo and the heroes of San Jacinto," the Rangers' story would "be enshrined in the hearts of Texans until time shall be merged in the twilight of eternity." Such protests, however, may indicate some insecurity about whether or not that truly would be the case.[38]

A number of factors undoubtedly influenced the abundance and the nature of the art that appeared at the Texas Capitol in the late nineteenth and early twentieth centuries. The construction of the building itself was, of course, a catalyst. In addition, the World's Columbian Exposition of 1893, widely attended by Texas citizens, created public demand for the beautification of spaces such as the Capitol grounds. Finally, the appearance of a handful of professional artists and institutions suggests that both affluence and population had reached the critical mass necessary for the development of a public art in the state. Yet none of these factors nor the traditions of European and American public art are enough to explain the overwhelming use of the theme of the "sturdy, stalwart Texan" in virtually every work of art at the Capitol.[39]

---

[37] Austin *Daily Statesman*, June 27, 1907.

[38] Cited in Cutrer's introduction to *A Terry Texas Ranger*, vi (1st and 2nd quotations); Austin *Daily Statesman*, June 27, 1907 (3rd and 4th quotations).

[39] Austin *Daily Statesman*, Apr. 26, 1891.

Significantly, at the same time that Huddle's and McArdle's paintings, Ney's statues, and the memorials to Texas Revolution and Civil War heroes appeared at the new Capitol, a number of organizations, such as the Texas State Historical Association, the United Daughters of the Confederacy, and the Daughters of the Republic of Texas, were organized in the state to study and preserve the region's history. Their appearance suggests what other social and economic factors also attest: that Texas, like the rest of the nation, was undergoing a major reorientation at the turn of the century. The commercialization of its agriculture, the movement toward industrialization, and the emerging dominance of urban over rural areas threatened the regional identity that many believed the state's founding fathers had tried to construct. Yet, at the same time, these developments promised an affluence that few members of the earlier generations had enjoyed. In that context, it is not surprising that the dominant culture gave visual expression to the ideal of the brave and self-reliant Texan. By showing "the rising generation the kind of men their fathers were," the Anglo-Texans who commissioned and sometimes created the art at the Texas Capitol were not only commemorating the past to instruct present and future Texans— they were also, perhaps, using the past to mediate the ambiguous and contradictory nature of their present experience.[40]

---

[40] Austin *Daily Statesman*, June 27, 1907 (quotation). For information on the social and political context of the 1890s, see Alwyn Barr, *Reconstruction to Reform: Texas Politics, 1876–1906* (Austin: University of Texas Press, 1971); for a discussion of the function of mythology and tradition in a conflicted culture, see Benedict, "Myth," and Eric Hobsbawm, "Introduction: Inventing Traditions," in Eric Hobsbawm and Terence Ranger (eds.), *The Invention of Tradition* (Cambridge: Cambridge University Press, 1983), 1–14.

Furnishing the Texas State Capitol

BONNIE ANN CAMPBELL*

> There was rejoicing written on the face of every legis-
> lator last night, and there was cause for such rejoic-
> ing; for it was the event of a life-time to be allowed the
> privilege of participating as a legislator in the chris-
> tening of the grandest state house in the union. . . .
> The empire state last night had placed upon it the
> everlasting seal of state unity.[1]

G REAT FANFARE ACCOMPANIED THE OFFICIAL OPENING OF THE NEWLY
completed Capitol in May, 1888. Contemporary newspaper accounts detailed the celebratory events—fireworks, drill exercises, a parade, and a grand ball. Glowing reports abounded, remarking upon
the grandeur and magnificence of the structure, "its vast proportions,
beautiful finish and skilled and artistic workmanship." No mention was
made however, of the interior furnishings—the draperies, carpeting,
and furniture. This was not due to oversight or lack of interest in such
details (indeed, many paragraphs were devoted merely to describing
the attire of various socialites at the ball). Interior descriptions were
lacking for quite a simple reason—no new interior furnishings were yet
in place to describe.[2]

---

*Bonnie Ann Campbell is the curator of the Texas Capitol, under the direction of the State
Preservation Board. Campbell was previously a curator at the California Capitol. The author
extends sincere appreciation and thanks to William Elton Green, capitol historian, for his research, generous assistance, and advice in the preparation of this paper. She would also like to
thank Sharon Darling, author of *Chicago Furniture: Art, Craft and Industry*, for sharing her extensive research notes, which are on file at the Chicago Historical Society.

[1] Austin *Daily Statesman*, May 11, 1888.

[2] Ibid., Mar. 1, 1888. Fortunately, the House of Representatives chamber, where the formal
ceremonies occurred on May 10, 1888, was not left barren. A resolution introduced by Representative William M. Skinner on May 11 thanked Gus Wilke (Capitol contractor) for moving
the old House of Representatives chamber furniture from the temporary capitol into the new
chamber at his own expense. *Journal of the House of Representatives of the Twentieth Legislature,
Extra Session, Begun and Held at Austin, Texas, April 16, 1888* (Austin: Hutchings Printing House,
1888), 215.

Although it was apparently a well-known fact that under the terms of the 1882 contract for the construction of the building the contractor was not required to furnish the rooms when completed (or to light the building or arrange the grounds), no attention seems to have been given to the furnishings until November, 1886. The *Third Biennial Report of the Capitol Building Commission* mentioned the need to furnish the building: "We have the reports upon a large number of capitol buildings in the various States, and also considerable data and other valuable information in regard to the kind of furniture used in other State houses."[3]

The commissioners' report must have spurred on the legislature. On March 1, 1887, Senator John M. Claiborne introduced Senate Bill 299, which primarily addressed furnishing the Capitol. Claiborne was chairman of a special joint committee established to decide, among other things, the course of action in furnishing the building.[4] The March 6, 1888, Austin *Daily Statesman* quoted the bill in full. A State Capitol Board was to be created, which would prepare a list of the type and amount of furniture and fixtures needed, advertise for bids for the items, and accept the lowest and best bidders. The bill provided $200,000 to carry out the requirements.[5]

On March 4, 1887, the Austin *Daily Statesman* printed a long and eloquently worded editorial in support of the legislation:

It seems to be a very necessary appropriation for a most obvious purpose. . . . It is foolishness to argue that the amount is too large. . . . This capitol will not only be the pride of the state of Texas but of this country, and it is only mete [*sic*] and proper that it should be furnished in a manner somewhat in conformity with the grandeur and magnificence of its appearance. If a wealthy man were to spend a large sum in erecting a dwelling, and then were to furnish it in a style no better than that adopted by a poor man, what would be the opinion of such an one?[6]

There may have been serious opposition to the amount of the appropriation, because two days later yet another strongly worded editorial

---

[3] *Third Biennial Report of the Capitol Building Commission . . . to the Governor of Texas, Austin, November 1, 1886* (Austin: Triplett & Hutchings, State Printers, 1886), 5. The information they amassed has apparently not survived.

[4] The committee was also to be responsible for arranging for the erection of porticoes originally designed for the west and east wings of the Capitol in accordance with the north portico then being built, improving the Capitol grounds, and purchasing two blocks of ground on the north side of the building to form a part of the Capitol grounds. *Senate Bill 299*, pp. 1–3, Engrossed and Printed Version, Twentieth Legislature, Regular Session, Records of the Legislature (RG 100), (Archives Division, Texas State Library, Austin).

[5] Austin *Daily Statesman*, Mar. 6, 1887.

[6] Ibid., Mar. 4, 1887.

focused on the wisdom of the bill. The article dismissed the idea that the furniture then being used in the temporary Capitol could be used in the new building: "Such furniture would be as unfit as putting the furniture of a third-rate hash house into the Driskill hotel." It was pointed out that other states had spent far more to furnish their Capitols, nearly all considerably smaller than the Texas building.[7] Should anyone suppose that the newspaper had a vested interest in the issue, the following statement concluded the column:

THE STATESMAN has no interest in this matter, save that pride which ought to animate and induce every newspaper and citizen of this great empire state . . . to urge . . . the manifest propriety of making adequate provisions . . . for suitably, substantially[,] and permanently furnishing this monumental structure.[8]

Claiborne's bill ended with an acknowledgment of the tardiness of the legislation: "Whereas . . . the new State Capitol building will be entirely completed and ready for occupancy at least six months before the next regular session of the Legislature, there is an imperative public necessity that the work . . . shall commence at once. . . ."[9] This injunction notwithstanding, the legislature did not approve the bill. While it passed the Senate, the legislation died in the House for an unknown reason, after successfully passing the House Finance Committee on March 19, 1887.[10]

One year later, similar legislation, House Bill 91, was introduced by Representative Jesse M. Strong on May 7, 1888, during the extra session of the Twentieth Legislature. This time, however, the $200,000 appropriated was expected to cover expenses for both the furnishings and fencing and ground improvements. During floor discussion on May 11, Representative William B. Page offered an amendment, which was approved, to reduce the appropriation from $200,000 to $140,000, with $100,000 allotted for furnishings and $40,000 for fencing and ground improvements.[11] The Austin *Daily Statesman* indicated its displeasure over this turn of events:

The joint committee of the two branches, upon the closest kind of an estimate, placed the amount required to suitably furnish the capitol at $150,000. The house, in a strained effort at a false economy, has cut it down to $100,000. Such

---

[7] Ibid., Mar. 6, 1887.

[8] Ibid.

[9] *Senate Bill 299*, p. 4, Engrossed and Printed Version, Twentieth Legislature, Regular Session.

[10] *Journal of the House of Representatives of the Twentieth Legislature, Begun and Held at the City of Austin, January 11, 1887* (Austin: Triplett & Hutchings, State Printers, 1887), 1,032.

[11] *Journal of the House of Representatives of the Twentieth Legislature, Extra Session*, 220.

action may be very acceptable to a backwoods constituency thoroughly un-
informed upon the merits of the case, but will scarcely find sanction among any
refined or well balanced people.[12]

The bill was sent to and passed by the Senate in record time, allowing
the governor to sign it into law on May 17, 1888.[13] Judging from the
proximity of the celebrations of the Capitol opening (May 14 to 19) to
the introduction, passage, and signing of the legislation, it is not far-
fetched to assume that the naked interior appearance of the building
was a bit disconcerting. It must have been abundantly clear to all concerned that something had to be done quickly to make the Capitol habitable. Habitable, but apparently not anything approaching grand,
since the legislators had reduced by one-half the initial appropriation
recommended in 1887. Not even the fervor associated with the grand
opening that month could loosen the purse strings of the traditionally
cost-conscious legislature.[14] Ever since the Democrats regained control
of the state at the end of Reconstruction in 1874, economy in government had been the prevailing principle. Even though a surplus existed
in the Treasury by the late 1880s, the politicians continued to stress
economy and practicality when considering appropriations.

The act for furnishing the Capitol went into effect on August 16,
1888. Four days later Governor Sul Ross appointed a three-member
Capitol Furnishing Board to contract for and oversee the installation of
furniture, floor coverings, and draperies. The members—William A.
Rhea of Collin County, William C. Holland of Dallas County, and
Rhoads Fisher of Travis County—met on August 25, at which time
Rhea was elected chairman and Fisher, secretary.[15]

The Capitol Furnishing Board asked all state officials and department heads to provide a list of the furniture required for their respective areas. The Austin *Daily Statesman* reported on September 1, 1888,

[12] Austin *Daily Statesman*, May 13, 1888.

[13] *Journal of the House of Representatives of the Twentieth Legislature, Extra Session*, 182–183,
217–222, 261; *General Laws of the State of Texas Passed at the Special Session of the Twentieth Legislature Convened at the City of Austin, April 16, 1888, and Adjourned May 15, 1888* (Austin: State
Printing Office, 1888), 14.

[14] The cost of Capitol furniture was not a new point of contention for the state. The furnishing of the 1850s Capitol became quite a subject of discussion. The *Report on the Building and
Furniture of the Capitol of the State of Texas* (Austin: Marshall & Oldham, State Printer, 1856)
details a dispute about the cost of the furnishings.

[15] *Report of the Capitol Furnishing Board* (Austin: Smith, Hicks & Jones, State Printers, 1889), 3.
Captain William Alexander Rhea had been a member of the legislature in 1864 and was appointed assistant adjutant general by Governor Pendleton Murrah. He served for three years
as president of the Ross Brigade Association of Ex-Confederates and was appointed by Governor John Ireland to the Farmers Congress. *Biographical Souvenir of the State of Texas . . .* (Chicago: F. A. Battery & Co., 1889), 717–718.

that the board had been in session for six days, reviewing the lists that had been submitted: "The Board has not been able to secure the services of such [a] furniture expert as is provided for by law. As early as this can be done satisfactorily the specifications will be made and advertisements inviting bids will be published. . . ."[16] According to the board's 1889 report, it hired Nicholas J. Clayton, a renowned architect from Galveston, to advise on the specifications.[17]

The advertisements for sealed proposals were published beginning September 26, 1888. The board's report indicates that it advertised in newspapers and to dealers, manufacturers, contractors, and others, both inside and outside Texas.[18] The bids were broken down into four categories, and the bidders could submit proposals for one or all of the categories.

1) Floor Coverings—consisting of Wiltons, Brussels, Rugs, Linoleum, Mattings, Etc.

2) Wooden Furniture—Chairs, Tables, Desks, Bookcases, Settees, Cuspidors, Opera Chairs, Clocks, Etc.

3) Iron and Steel Furniture—Roller Shelving, Document Files, Pigeonholes, Vault Fixtures

4) Draperies—Curtains, Fringes, and Other Ornaments.[19]

The detailed lists and specifications were available to bidders at the board's office after September 17, 1888. Bids, including delivery and placement in the rooms, would be accepted until October 27 and opened October 29.[20]

The first contracts were not awarded until November 3. According to the Austin *Daily Statesman*, hundreds of bids were submitted, "and it will probably require several days to foot them up and single out the lowest and best. . . ."[21] A $25,500 contract for the iron and steel furniture was given to the American Shelf and Drawer Company of Chicago (later renamed the Fenton Metalic [*sic*] and Manufacturing Com-

---

[16] Austin *Daily Statesman*, Sept. 1, 1888.

[17] *Report of the Capitol Furnishing Board*, 3. Clayton arrived at Galveston from Memphis, Tennessee, in 1872. He advertised that he was the earliest established professional architect in the state. Clayton received many important commissions in the late nineteenth century, including commercial buildings, schools, churches, and homes. St. Mary's Cathedral and St. Edward's University are two Austin landmarks designed by Clayton. Walter Prescott Webb, H. Bailey Carroll, and Eldon Stephen Branda (eds.), *The Handbook of Texas* (3 vols.; Austin: Texas State Historical Association, 1952, 1976), III, 175.

[18] *Report of the Capitol Furnishing Board*, 4.

[19] Austin *Daily Statesman*, Sept. 26, 1888.

[20] Ibid.

[21] Ibid., Oct. 31, 1888.

pany of Chicago). All of the departmental requests for this type of furniture were filled, except for half of the burglar- and fireproof Treasury boxes used for storing money and bonds. The metallic furniture was to be installed by March 28, 1889.[22]

Contracts totaling $23,000 for floor coverings and draperies were also awarded on November 3 to A. H. Andrews and Company of Chicago. Some confusion apparently existed over the awarding of the draperies contract. On November 8, 1889, the Austin *Daily Statesman* reported that the contract for draperies, totaling approximately $25,000, had been given to Marshall Field and Company of Chicago. The sum of the contract was close to the total amount previously reported by the newspaper for both the draperies and floor covering contracts, which it earlier said had been awarded to Andrews. The following day the paper stated that the draperies contract had gone to Andrews. The board's 1889 report lists Andrews as having received the contracts for floor coverings and draperies, which would seem to put an end to the matter. In January, 1889, however, the Austin *Daily Statesman* noted that Furnishing Board member Fisher had received a telegram from Marshall Field and Company informing him that all the floor coverings for the new Capitol, except those for the Senate chamber, Hall of Representatives, and Supreme Courtroom, had been shipped.[23] Perhaps the confusion can be explained if it is assumed that while Andrews received the contract for the floor coverings and draperies, it was well known that the firm was going to subcontract the supply of the materials to Marshall Field and Company, a major department store. There is no evidence that Andrews directly manufactured draperies or floor coverings.

The major furnishings contract, totaling approximately $50,000 for wood furniture, was likewise awarded to the Andrews firm on November 7, 1889. The Austin *Daily Statesman* reported that Andrews was "among the largest dealers in the United States and in about ten days will have samples on exhibition at the capitol of their goods. They would be pleased at that time to have every lady in Austin to visit their display."[24]

The report of the Furnishing Board noted that the wood furniture had to be made according to specifications of the U.S. government. Since this type of furniture was not kept in stock by companies, each piece had to be specially manufactured. Therefore, the Capitol would not be

[22] *Report of the Capitol Furnishing Board*, 6.
[23] Austin *Daily Statesman*, Nov. 4, 8, 9, 1888, Jan. 15, 1889.
[24] Austin *Daily Statesman*, Nov. 9, 1888.

ready for the convening of the Twenty-first Legislature in January. The Senate and House chambers were to be furnished by February 23, 1889, and all other furniture was to arrive no later than April 6, 1889.[25]

Remembering that the amount of funding had been reduced by one-half, it is not surprising that the report stated that the board could not purchase everything requested for the Capitol. The board eventually decided to furnish some areas totally and other areas not at all, leaving the latter to await future appropriations.[26] Department heads and leading members of the legislature were not spared, as can be seen from the following list of spaces left unfurnished:

1st floor: treasurer's private room, comptroller's private room, attorney general's reception room, Department of Education reception room

2nd floor: governor's two consultation rooms, president of the senate's private room, Speaker's private room

3rd floor: 8 Senate committee rooms, 7 House committee rooms, reporter's private office

4th floor: 9 halls and 13 rooms, not assigned to any departments.[27]

By early December the final decisions about exact styles of furniture had been made, and patterns of draperies, fabric, and carpeting had been selected. The Austin *Daily Statesman* praised the work of the members of the Furnishing Board:

They have displayed remarkably good taste in their selections and wisdom has guided them in fixing the price of the various articles. No extravagant prices have been paid, nor have flimsy materials been selected. . . . No better selections could have been made, and the capitol will be furnished in keeping with its style and the grandeur of the building.[28]

Echoing the tone of the *Statesman*'s comment, the board concluded its report with a subtle plea that the legislature furnish the Capitol completely and appropriately:

While the Board . . . feels confident that it will get full value for all the money expended, it believes that it reflects the wishes of the people in its desire to furnish the capitol in a style commensurate with the dignity and wealth of their State, and in harmony with the architectural beauty and grandeur of the building.[29]

---

[25] *Report of the Capitol Furnishing Board,* 7.

[26] Ibid.

[27] Ibid. It is not clear when funds were appropriated to furnish these areas.

[28] Austin *Daily Statesman,* Dec. 8, 1888.

[29] *Report of the Capitol Furnishing Board,* 9.

The furniture for the Senate and House chambers arrived early in February. "The desks are large, roomy and splendidly arranged, and are very handsome. The chairs are strong, beautiful and comfortable. Those for the House are of oak, while those intended for the Senate chamber are of walnut. A carload or two of furniture is expected this morning."[30]

By July, 1889, all of the new Capitol furnishings must have arrived, because an auction of the old furniture previously used in the building was announced for early August.[31] The Capitol was, for the most part, finally furnished. A full year after being officially opened to the public, the building was now functional and even more worthy of the hyperbolic praise it had received during the preceding few years.

What draperies, floor coverings, and furniture were purchased for the Capitol? Three primary sources exist to help answer the question: copies of the original specifications provided to bidders, early historical photographs, and surviving examples of original furniture.

While it cannot be determined if everything included in the specifications was provided, it can be assumed that, for the most part, the requirements were met. A general examination of the twenty-eight-page *Specifications for Furnishing the New Capitol of Texas* reveals a great deal about the original ambience of the Capitol interiors. The overall impression is that, with few exceptions, only the basic, functional needs of the various legislative and state departments were fulfilled. The section titled "General Specifications" (listed on page 27) indicates a primary concern for quality materials. While it may not have favored ostentation, the board clearly wanted items that would serve the state long and well. Everything was to conform to U.S. government regulations; glass was to be "double strength"; mirrors, only French plate (a particular quality of mirror) with a beveled edge; carpeting, the best five-frame available—and samples and patterns were to be submitted for all items. Even the smallest details were not overlooked: "The castors for all articles of furniture requiring castors must be of the approved pattern, and of the best material."[32]

Draperies were to be used sparingly. Only sixteen rooms were originally scheduled to be fitted with window draperies (there were also rostrum draperies in the House and Senate chambers and the Supreme Courtroom). Seven of the rooms were public reception areas and were

---

[30] Austin *Daily Statesman*, Feb. 8, 1889.

[31] Ibid., July 28, 1889.

[32] *Specifications for Furnishing the New Capitol of Texas*, Capitol Furnishing Board (n.p., [1888]), 27, copy in Manuscript Collection (Archives Division, Texas State Library, Austin).

probably considered comparable to parlors, which traditionally had draperies. A few "private rooms," or offices, were also to have draperies: those of the governor, comptroller, and Department of Education. Interestingly, the private rooms of the Speaker and the president of the Senate were to receive only the standard shutters, although draperies were specified for the nonprivate rooms of these officials. It is difficult to understand why the comptroller and director of the Department of Education would have received draperies in their private rooms while the legislative leaders, secretary of state, Supreme Court justices, treasurer, and attorney general were all denied this amenity.[33]

Cost estimates for draperies were included in the Andrews bid and provide further information about the quality, or elaborateness, of draperies deemed appropriate for each room. The draperies behind the Senate and House rostrums were to cost $225 each, and those behind the Supreme Court dais, $125. Sixty dollars was the estimate per window for the public rooms belonging to the treasurer, attorney general, and Department of Education; $85 was quoted for the Speaker's and the president of the Senate's rooms; the comptroller merited $125 draperies. In the governor's area the cost increased to $200 per window, while the Governor's public reception room (considered the most special room in the building) topped the list at $350 per window.[34]

The distribution of floor coverings also suggests that there was an understood hierarchy within state government. The floor coverings can be divided into three categories: carpeting and rugs, linoleum, and matting. Fifty-nine rooms were to receive carpeting or rugs. "Body Brussels" carpeting was specified for fifty-four of these rooms. Only five rooms, all in the executive (governor's) department, were to receive "Royal Wilton" carpeting.[35]

Body Brussels and Wilton carpeting were very popular in America during the last quarter of the nineteenth century. Considered extremely long-wearing, they were constructed nearly identically and woven on the same type of loom. The only variation was that the Brussels style had a looped-pile, whereas the loop in the Wilton variety was cut, creating a cut-pile or "velvety" surface. A late nineteenth-century taste-maker remarked that body Brussels was "a universal sort of carpet, not

---

[33] Note that five of the rooms that were to receive draperies ultimately were not furnished: the governor's consultation rooms (two), attorney general's reception room, Department of Education reception room, and comptroller's private room. *Report of the Capitol Furnishing Board*, 7.

[34] *Specifications for Furnishing the New Capitol of Texas*, Exhibit D, 1, 3, 4, 9, 11, 12, 14, 17, 19, 21.

[35] Ibid., Exhibit C (Andrews), 1–4, 9, 11–14, 17–19, 21, 23–24.

too rich for the poor, not too poor for the rich." Despite the similarity of construction, Wiltons were considerably more expensive than body Brussels carpets. The carpet bids completed by Andrews quoted the Brussels carpeting at $1.50 a yard, versus $3.33 a yard for Wilton. Although the body Brussels carpet cost less than half of what the Wilton did, it was far more expensive than other types of Brussels carpet, all of which were of lesser quality. The Furnishing Board could have specified a tapestry Brussels, for instance, which would have cost one-half as much as a body Brussels carpet.[36]

The Andrews bid did not indicate which manufacturers were to supply the Capitol's carpeting. As suggested earlier, Marshall Field and Company was probably Andrews's source. Apparently Marshall Field and Company had direct access to a carpet mill, since an unsuccessful bidder, Rhea Osborne, specified Marshall Field and Company patterns several times in its bid. Two other manufacturers cited frequently in Osborne's bid were Lowell and Bigelow, the primary American firms providing Brussels and Wilton carpeting in the late nineteenth century. The 1878 *Proposals for Carpets and Linoleum for the New Capitol of Michigan* required the use of Wiltons produced by either Lowell or Bigelow, and Brussels produced by either Lowell, Bigelow, or one of three other firms. While Marshall Field and Company may have supplied the Capitol's carpeting, it very well could have ordered much of it from the Lowell or Bigelow firms, particularly given the deadline under which it was forced to operate.[37]

Printed (as opposed to plain) linoleum was specified for nearly all of the remaining rooms in the Capitol. For the House and Senate galleries, special wording informed the bidders that the floors were to be covered with the "best quality of linoleum." All other references to linoleum simply stated "linoleum on floor." There were several grades of linoleum available in the late 1880s: "Double Extra Thick," "Extra Thick," "Royal," and "A." It is unclear from the bid documents which grades Andrews quoted for the Capitol. However, it quoted eighty-five cents a yard for the House and Senate galleries and ninety cents a yard for all the other linoleum, which suggests that it did not notice (or

---

[36] Gail Caskey Winkler and Roger W. Moss, *Victorian Interior Decoration: American Interiors, 1830–1900* (New York: Henry Holt & Co., 1986), 153. In body Brussels carpet, colored yarns were woven to form a pattern. In a tapestry Brussels, specific areas of the strands of yarn were dyed to create the pattern.

[37] *Specifications for Furnishing the New Capitol of Texas*, Exhibit C (Osborne); *Proposals for Carpets and Linoleum for the New Capitol of Michigan at Lansing* (n.p., n.d.), copy in O. A. Jenison Manuscript Collection (6 vols. of scrapbooks; Library of Michigan, Detroit), VI, n.p.

heed) the board's implied desire that the gallery linoleum be of a better grade than that in the remainder of the Capitol.[38]

Linoleum was invented in 1863 by the English india-rubber manufacturer Frederick Walton. It was considered a less expensive floor covering than either carpeting or encaustic tile, both of which were imitated by linoleum patterns. Derived from the latin *linum* (flax) and *oleum* (oil), nineteenth-century linoleum was made from dried, shredded, and powdered linseed oil that was combined with ground cork or sawdust, pigments, and gums, then forced under pressure onto a burlap backing. It was first manufactured in the United States in 1869 by the New York–based American Linoleum Manufacturing Company. In 1886 a New Jersey competitor began operations under the name of the Nairn factory.[39] The Andrews bid did not refer to a particular brand; however, Osborne proposed in its bid that all linoleum should be "Scotch Royal, width 4 yards, Nairns make, 904 [yards] figured, 804 [yards] plain."[40]

Matting was the least expensive floor covering used throughout the nineteenth century. Usually made of grass and hemp, it remained fairly popular in the 1880s, being used primarily as a protective covering for carpets. Basic matting ranged between fifteen cents and fifty cents a yard. Japanese matting, considered a superior product, had a grass weft and a cotton warp and was priced from fifty cents to a dollar a yard.[41] The "General Specifications" for furnishing the Capitol noted that cocoa, Japanese, or any other good matting could be used. Very little matting was actually specified. The two consultation rooms and the two private offices of the governor were to have doormats, as were the business and the private secretary's office. The only other mats specified were two rubber mats for the Department of Education. The Andrews quotes for the grass matting were fifty-eight cents a yard and seventy-four cents a yard. The Osborne firm quoted prices for additional matting that it recommended for various locations: at each entrance of the building; at the foot of each staircase; outside the Supreme Courtroom and the governor's public reception room (the latter to be trimmed with a woolen border); and at the entrances to the

---

[38] *Specifications for Furnishing the New Capitol of Texas*, Exhibit C (Andrews), 1–4, 9, 11, 13–14, 16, 18, 20–22, 24–27.

[39] Helene Von Rosenstiel, *American Rugs and Carpeting* (New York: William Morrow & Co., 1978), 62–63.

[40] *Specifications for Furnishing the New Capitol of Texas*, Exhibit C (Osborne), on reverse of 1.

[41] Winkler and Moss, *Victorian Interior Decoration*, 198–199.

House and Senate chambers (to be lettered; presumably: "House of Representatives" and "Senate Chamber").[42]

While draperies and floor coverings were important components of the furnishings for the Capitol, primary emphasis was necessarily placed on the furniture required for the massive building. More than 75 percent of the $100,000 furnishings budget was allotted to furniture. A quick addition finds that over 1,100 chairs alone were listed in the *Specifications,* not including settees, gallery seating, or lounges. Analysis of the *Specifications* does not reveal anything unexpected in terms of what was requested. Rooms were to be furnished with flat-top, curtain (rolltop), or standing desks; straight leg, rotary (swivel), or platform rocking chairs; stationary or revolving bookcases; tables; file cabinets; wardrobes; clocks; and spittoons or cuspidors.[43]

Private rooms were distinguished only by the more frequent appearance of lounges or wardrobes. A few private rooms (Speaker, president of the Senate, and their corresponding chief clerks) were also to receive washstands, complete with cabinet, basin, towel racks, and mirror, perhaps an indication that these men were expected to spend many long hours at the Capitol and would need to freshen up from time to time. The only rooms in the building for which beds were specified were in the judiciary department. The ten beds for the judges were to be a folding variety with mirrored fronts, undoubtedly so that during the day the rooms would have more space and would reflect an office— rather than a bedroom—environment.[44]

In general, the expected hierarchy is reflected in the type or cost of furnishings supplied for the various departments. Unfortunately, the Andrews furniture bids have not survived, but those of an unsuccessful bidder, the Robert Mitchell Furniture Company, still exist. Although the prices may not be the same ones quoted by Andrews, they undoubt-

---

[42] *Specifications for Furnishing the New Capitol of Texas,* Exhibit C (Osborne), 23 and reverse.

[43] It should be noted that the legislators originally did not have individual offices in the Capitol. A desk on the chamber floor was the extent of one's "office." It was not until the 1940s that senators had offices in the Capitol; House members received offices there in the 1960s.

[44] Each judge on the Supreme Court and the Commission of Appeals was to receive a washstand, furniture that would be expected in a room meant to function as a bedroom as well as an office. Offices for the Court of Appeals judges and assistant attorney general, while furnished with beds, received no washstands.

An 1884 law had barred legislative members and other state officials from sleeping in the Capitol; judicial members were exempted, however. Apparently members did not always respect the restriction. A March 4, 1895, article in the *Statesman* discussed the problem of members' sleeping in committee rooms: "When strangers are admiring our beautiful capitol the sentiment is knocked out of them to see red blankets and soiled sheets aired in its windows." On February 24, 1897, the *Statesman* noted that when Superintendent John R. Mobley took charge of the building two years earlier, he had found eighty beds in the Capitol. In 1897 Mobley stopped the practice by refusing to allow members' luggage to be admitted into the building.

Figure 1. Governor Samuel Willis Tucker Lanham seated at his desk, c. 1905. *Courtesy Barker Texas History Center, University of Texas at Austin.*

edly reflect the relative degrees of quality and design that were planned for the various rooms.

For example, curtain desks were reserved for the primary state officials: the governor's area; comptroller; treasurer; secretary of state; attorney general; and so forth. A further hierarchy can be determined by the prices Mitchell quoted for these desks: $63.00 for the janitor, state geologist, agriculture and insurance commissioner, treasurer, governor's business office; $82.50 for the adjutant general, Department of Education, attorney general, secretary of state, and comptroller; and $165.00 for the governor's model.[45]

A photograph of Governor S. W. T. Lanham circa 1903–1907 includes his curtain desk (fig. 1). When one compares this photograph to pictures that illustrate the other types of curtain desks supplied for the building (see fig. 9), it is clear that the governor's desk is a superior grade, containing carved drawers and a spindle gallery around the upper section. A nearly identical desk, now in the collection of the Chicago Historical Society, was once owned by Marshall Field, one of the

[45] *Specifications for Furnishing the New Capitol of Texas,* Exhibit titled "Robert Mitchell Furniture Co.," 11, 14, 17–19, 21, 23–26.

most prominent citizens in the U.S. in the last decades of the nineteenth century.[46]

Thousands and thousands of individual items of office furniture were required for the Capitol. The legislation that established the Capitol Furnishing Board originally instructed the members to advertise for proposals in Chicago, St. Louis, Cincinnati, and various Texas cities.[47] Yet there was no possibility that a Texas manufacturer could have supplied the necessary furniture. According to 1890 U.S. census figures, only thirty-eight firms in the entire state of Texas were devoted to furniture making, cabinetmaking, and upholstering, with a total annual product of $161,231. In comparison, one Chicago firm alone sold over $1.5 million worth of products in 1885.[48]

Many people have assumed that the Huntsville penitentiary supplied a great deal of the original Capitol furniture. The penitentiaries have a long history of providing furniture to the state. The original 1887 furnishings legislation included a reference to the penitentiary furniture factories:

the board may have as much of this furniture made at the penitentiary as they may feel assured the penitentiary authorities can make equal, in every respect, in style, workmanship and price, as that proposed by other bidders . . . and if any of the said furniture should be made at the penitentiaries it shall be the duty of the proper penitentiary officers to keep a special itemized statement of the account . . . and to report the same to the Governor.[49]

There is no indication in either the 1890 or 1892 superintendent of state penitentiaries biennial reports that the penitentiaries supplied any original furniture to the Capitol.[50]

---

[46] The present location of the original governor's desk is unknown; we know, however, that it was still in the building as late as 1929. A January 22, 1929, *Statesman* article announced that "the massive walnut desk and table used from the time of Governor Hogg to Governor [Pat M.] Neff [which were] carved, and of great historic interest," were to be auctioned along with other discarded furniture from the Capitol. The next day the paper reported that the Board of Control had changed its mind and would keep the desk and table in the Capitol.

[47] *Journal of the House of Representatives of the Twentieth Legislature, Extra Session*, 182, 217. The city of Cincinnati may have been specified so as to alert the Robert Mitchell Furniture Company to the job. Mitchell supplied the furniture for the 1886 Driskill hotel. Austin *Daily Statesman*, Dec. 17, 1886.

[48] U.S., Department of the Interior, Census Office, *Compendium of the Eleventh Census: 1890* (3 vols.; Washington, D.C.: Government Printing Office, 1894–1897), III, 840–841; A. T. Andreas, *History of Chicago: 1871–1885* (3 vols.; Chicago: A. T. Andreas Co., 1886), II, 735.

[49] *Senate Bill 299*, p. 2 (three-page version), Twentieth Legislature, Regular Session, RG 100 (Archives Division, Texas State Library, Austin).

[50] In 1903, however, the *Statesman* reported that the "elegant oak furniture" for the newly created Railroad Commission hearing room was strictly a Texas product. "It was manufactured in the Huntsville penitentiary. . . . The workmanship is in the very highest style . . . and would be creditable in style, design and finish to any furniture factory in the United States." Austin *Daily Statesman*, Dec. 9 (1st quotation), 17 (2nd quotation), 1903.

The sheer volume of furnishings needed made it almost a certainty that a Chicago firm would receive the contract. By the 1880s Chicago was one of the largest cities in the nation. Between 1871, when a fire destroyed the majority of the city, and 1893 Chicago experienced a phenomenal building boom: in twenty-two years nearly 99,000 buildings were constructed in the city, all needing to be furnished. By 1885 Chicago was considered the leading furniture manufacturing center in the country, both in numbers of employees and in the amount of annual product.[51]

The largest Chicago firm engaged in the manufacture of commercial furniture in the 1880s and 1890s was A. H. Andrews and Company, with branches in New York, Philadelphia, and Boston. Established in 1865, the firm produced a wide variety of furniture and obtained many important commercial commissions, including the Hartford, Connecticut, post office; the Customs House in Chicago; the Cook County courthouse; the Philadelphia courthouse and post office; the Administration Building for the 1893 World's Columbian Exposition in Chicago; and the Chicago Public Library. Andrews had also supplied furniture for other capitols, including Michigan's in 1878, and had shipped products to Texas previous to the Capitol contract. One known instance occurred in 1883–1884, when the firm supplied the furniture for the Shackelford County courthouse in Albany.[52]

Certain items specified for the Capitol were furnishings that Andrews was particularly well suited to provide. Besides the hundreds of desks, tables, and other items illustrated in its catalogues, Andrews was renowned for certain innovative patent furniture, such as folding beds and opera (or gallery) chairs. According to 1880s advertisements, Andrews had over twenty styles of folding beds to select from when the Capitol specifications were issued, requiring ten such beds for the judges' rooms. One hundred Andrews folding beds were used in the Palmer House, Chicago's premier hotel, built in the 1880s.[53]

The specifications for the gallery seating in the chambers called for "iron opera chairs, [with] folding seats, and perforated backs and bottoms." Andrews had been manufacturing opera chairs since the early 1870s; an 1886 catalogue boasts of thirty available styles—plain, perforated, or upholstered. Andrews opera chairs were placed in most of

---

[51] Sharon Darling, *Chicago Furniture: Art, Craft and Industry, 1833–1983* (New York: Chicago Historical Society and W. W. Norton & Co., 1984), 45, 122.

[52] Ibid., 124–125; Lansing *Republican*, Jan. 17, 31, 1878; Willard B. Robinson, *Texas Public Buildings of the Nineteenth Century* (Austin: University of Texas Press for the Amon Carter Museum of Western Art, 1974), 228.

[53] Darling, *Chicago Furniture*, 127.

Figure 2. This lock, which reads "A. H. Andrews & Co/Mnfg/Chicago," is found on many pieces of Capitol furniture. *Courtesy John Anderson.*

Chicago's many theaters, as well as in several New York establishments, including the Metropolitan Opera House and the Bijou. In 1889 the firm received the largest contract ever awarded at that time for opera chairs—4,000 for Chicago's Auditorium Theater. (The Capitol, in comparison, required approximately 1,400 opera chairs.)[54]

Several historical photographs exist that give a fair impression of some of the Capitol's original draperies and floor coverings. Documentation of original Capitol furniture is even more conclusive, for not only photographs but actual examples have survived. A recent Capitol inventory uncovered nearly 200 objects that can be firmly documented as original furniture.[55] Documentation is based upon photographic comparisons and, in many cases, original labels or company marks.

A large department within the Andrews operations was solely devoted to fine brass work. Advertisements note that the company manufactured all its own brass, including the railings, gates, partitions, and screens needed for the many banks it furnished. Andrews also made all of its own locks and, fortunately, displayed mastery of the metal by

---

[54] *Specifications for Furnishing the New Capitol of Texas,* 1, 3; Darling, *Chicago Furniture,* 126.

[55] This figure does not include the 181 members' desks in the chambers. Many more original Capitol furnishings exist in other state office buildings, museums, and private collections, and are in the process of being inventoried.

Figure 3. Original Capitol settee. *Courtesy John Anderson.*

creating elaborately decorated mechanisms that included its name. Many desks, tables, bookcases, wardrobes, and washstands in the Capitol can be documented as Andrews pieces thanks to the existence of these beautiful locks (fig. 2).[56]

While Andrews manufactured a great deal of the Capitol furniture, the company also purchased many items from other firms. This was not an unusual practice, particularly when an extremely large contract had to be completed in short order. Surviving labels and maker's marks reveal that J. S. Ford, Johnson and Company of Chicago and the Milwaukee Chair Company were two firms that supplied furniture, via Andrews, to the Capitol.

A brass plate located on one of the few remaining original settees reads: "J. S. Ford, Johnson and Co. / Manufacturers Chicago, Ill." (fig. 3). Eight such settees, with "Perforated backs and bottoms, about 6 feet long, for 3 persons each, with divisions," were specified for the Supreme Court. Settees were also specified for the perimeter of the main floor of the House and Senate chambers; these, however, were to be upholstered in leather. No leather examples have survived; nor are any

---

[56] Darling, *Chicago Furniture*, 127; advertisement in *Chicago Business Directory* (n.p., n.d.), n.p. (obtained from personal research files of Sharon Darling, stored at Chicago Historical Society; no identification for source included on xerox of page).

Figure 4. Texas House of Representatives chamber in the late nineteenth century. The white lines criss-crossing the photograph are ropes which were sometimes used to support a tarp that covered the chamber to cut out some of the
sunlight admitted by the glass skylight. *Courtesy Barker Texas History Center, University of Texas at Austin.*

settees visible in any of the early chamber photographs. A settee included in the 1878 *Proposals for Furniture for the New Capitol of Michigan
at Lansing* is similar to a scaled drawing of the desired leather settee and
matching chair that appears in the *Specifications.* A Lansing *Republican*
newspaper article lists Andrews & Co. as having received the contract
for the "settees in the galleries, polygon desks, and other furniture."[57]
Perhaps Andrews suggested the design to Ford as a model to follow for
Texas (or perhaps Ford made the Michigan settees as well). The Texas
example is noticeably simpler in decoration, due in part, no doubt, to
budgetary restrictions, and possibly to a change in stylistic preference
over the intervening ten years.

Among the several styles of rotary chairs in the Capitol, the swivel
mechanisms of two are stamped "J. S. F. J. and Co. Patent." Several examples of one of the chairs are visible in a late nineteenth-century
photograph of the House chamber (fig. 4). The chairs are arranged behind the back two rows of desks. It is possible that these chairs were

[57] *Specifications for Furnishing the New Capitol of Texas,* 5; Lansing *Republican,* Jan. 17, 1878.

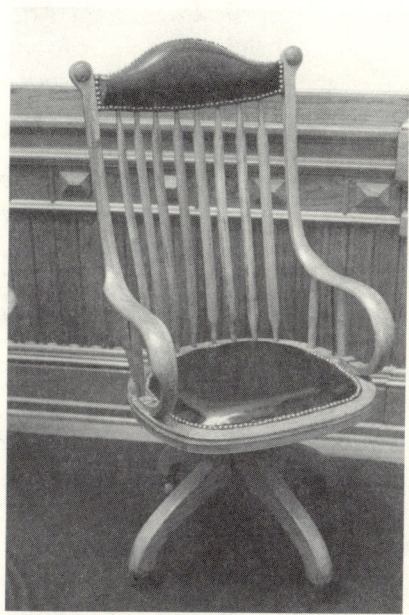 

Figure 5. Two surviving chairs like those seen in various historical photographs taken in the Capitol. *Courtesy John Anderson.*

purchased in the early 1890s for the twenty-two members who were added at that time to the House of Representatives.[58]

J. S. Ford, Johnson and Company was, like Andrews, one of the leading manufacturers of the period. For years its logo was "J. S. Ford, Johnson and Company / Manufacturers of Chairs and Settees." In the mid-1880s it was said to have 3,000 varieties of chairs available to buyers. The *American Furniture Gazette* declared that the company had "probably the most varied assortment offered by any one house in America." In 1893 it received what must have been its largest order: 54,000 chairs for the dedication exercises at the World's Columbian Exposition. Despite the company's large volume of production, Ford found it necessary to supplement its manufacture with chairs from several other firms in order to meet the deadline.[59]

[58] *Members of the Texas Legislature, 1846–1980* (Austin: Texas Senate, 1980), 147–151. A count of the House members listed for the Twenty-third Legislature, 1893, totals 128. The count for the twenty-first Legislature, 1889, when the Capitol was being furnished, totals 106. See pages 131–134.

[59] Copies of the company's stationery between 1887 and 1894 include this logo. Obtained from Sharon Darling's personal research files (Chicago Historical Society). Cited in Darling, *Chicago Furniture*, 115–116.

Nearly 600 perforated chairs were included in the Capitol furnishings specifications.[60] The majority of the historical photographs of Capitol interiors show at least one of these chairs in the pictured room (fig. 5). Surviving examples reveal three types of perforated chairs: a side and an arm version, both with five holes in the crest rail, and an armchair with a solid crest rail decorated with low-relief leaf carving. Although dozens of these chairs still exist, none have labels or maker's marks. It is tempting to assume they were made by J. S. Ford, Johnson and Company for three major reasons: the perforated pattern, a star within a shield, is the same as that found on the settees; the firm was famous for its chairs and could fill a large order very easily; and a documented Ford chair in the collection of the Chicago Historical Society is extremely similar. An 1886 Andrews catalogue, however, illustrated a chair that is also very similar.[61] Andrews could have duplicated the perforated design found on the settees. A conclusive answer will have to await further evidence.

Early photographs of the Senate and House chambers document the original swivel chairs used by the members at their desks (see figs. 4 and 7). A few of these chairs still remain in the Capitol, kept in offices more as artifacts than as functional objects. The swivel mechanisms are stamped: "Milwaukee Chair Co." According to an 1886 *Industrial History of Milwaukee,* the firm was one of the largest manufacturing establishments in the city. "The specialty of this firm is office and other styles of fine chairs, which have won for this house a national reputation." By 1890 its business had expanded to include international clients. The *Illustrated Annual Review of Milwaukee: Its Trade and Industries* claimed that "the management holds the manufacture exclusively to the finest chairs on the market." In 1910 the Milwaukee Chair Company supplied chairs used in the new wings of the Wisconsin State Capitol.[62]

In February, 1889, the Austin *Daily Statesman* reported that the newly arrived chairs were "strong, beautiful and comfortable."[63] A few years later when the new members were added to the House of Representatives, an attempt was apparently made to purchase chairs to match the originals. According to the 1892 *Biennial Report of the Superintendent of Public Buildings and Grounds:*

---

[60] This figure was arrived at by adding up all the perforated chairs listed in the twenty-eight-page *Specifications.*

[61] A. H. Andrews and Company, *Commercial Furniture* (Chicago: n.p., 1886), 60.

[62] *Industrial History of Milwaukee* (Milwaukee: E. E. Barton, 1886), 209; *Illustrated Annual Review of Milwaukee: Its Trade and Industries* (Milwaukee: Milwaukee Sentinel, 1890), 133; Anne Woodhouse, "Manufactured Furniture from Wisconsin," *Wisconsin Academy Review,* XXX (Mar., 1984), 57, 58.

[63] Austin *Daily Statesman,* Feb. 8, 1889.

Figure 6. The Senate chamber, c. 1910. *Courtesy Austin History Center, Austin Public Library.*

The legislature passed a resolution requiring the Superintendent . . . to buy desks and chairs for the 22 extra members. . . . The chairs purchased were burned in the Great Milwaukee fire, and it was too late to get the bill duplicated; had to take chairs of a different make.[64]

The Milwaukee Chair Company was certainly the intended supplier.

What were the overall results of House Bill 91, the legislation that established the Capitol Furnishing Board and provided $100,000 for the purchase of draperies, floor coverings, and furniture for the new building? Analysis of early photographs of selected rooms in the Capitol will help to consolidate the information discussed in the preceding pages.

An early twentieth-century view of the Senate chamber documents many of the items listed in the 1888 *Specifications* (fig. 6). The provision for "Draperies, etc., suitable for President's platform; $225.00" materialized as a back curtain and triple-swagged and cascaded front drapery arrangement, trimmed with a six-inch tassel and bullion fringe. The

[64] *Report of Superintendent of Public Buildings and Grounds, Austin, November 1, 1892* (Austin: Ben C. Jones & Co., State Printers, 1892), 4.

Figure 7. Photograph of the Senate chamber in 1901. *Courtesy Austin History Center, Austin Public Library.*

style of arrangement and trimming was very popular during the late Victorian period. Identical draperies are seen in early House chamber photographs as well (see fig. 4).[65]

The "best-quality five-frame Brussels carpeting" seen in the photograph, the second carpet used in the chamber, was installed by 1902. Both it and the original carpet (fig. 7) correspond to the style favored during the last decades of the nineteenth-century. The large-scale, elaborate rococo pattern popular in the 1860s had been gradually replaced by smaller-scale, restrained patterns that were generally less naturalistic and more stylized. Charles L. Eastlake, the leading influence on Victorian taste in the late 1800s, believed that carpet patterns should be "simple, good design[s] free of ostentatious ornamentation" and suggested that the "quaint and curious" designs found in ancient tiles be imitated. Small designs laid in a diapered pattern (similar to the Senate carpeting circa 1902) were often recommended by Eastlake and other late Victorian tastemakers. Although hard to discern in the black-

---

[65] *Specifications for Furnishing the New Capitol of Texas*, Exhibit D, 1. A 1986 interim restoration project in the House chamber exactingly reproduced the rich draperies and trimming. See Bonnie Ann Campbell, "Restoration of the State Capitol," *Heritage*, V (Spring, 1987), 24–27.

and-white photograph, the colors in the carpetings probably also conformed to late nineteenth-century preferences. The vibrant colors favored in earlier decades were exchanged for more muted tones of maroon, mushroom, rust, and grayed blues, golds, and browns. Very few whites or primary colors were used.[66]

Much of the furniture listed in the *Specifications* can be seen in the photograph. Members' chairs were to have a plain leather seat and back. The chairs that were provided had a three-quarter upholstered seat, and only the crest rail of the back was upholstered. Likewise, the *Specifications* included an upholstered chair for the president of the Senate. The chair visible in the photograph has an eight-slat wooden back. The present location of the chair is not known, so it cannot be determined if at least the seat was upholstered. The president's desk, the secretary of the Senate's standing desk, and one of the three sitting desks specified for the chamber are visible in the photograph. The sitting desk (now used at the back of the chamber as an information desk) contains Andrews locks. Since the design and carving of all of the sitting desks are identical, it can be assumed that they are all Andrews products. Other photographs document the leather armchairs specified for guests (such as secretaries) on the chamber floor. These chairs generally seem to be straight-leg versions of the members' rotary chairs.[67]

The "iron opera chairs, folding seats, and perforated backs and bottoms" listed in the *Specifications* are seen in the gallery and have the general appearance of advertised Andrews examples. The Robert Mitchell Furniture Company's unsuccessful bid quoted each chair at $2.75. If the Andrews price was comparable, the Senate gallery seating would have cost approximately $1,800.[68]

---

[66] *Specifications for Furnishing the New Capitol of Texas*, 1 (1st quotation); Winkler and Moss, *Victorian Interior Decoration*, 154 (2nd quotation), 155 (3rd quotation); Von Rosenstiel, *American Rugs and Carpeting*, 122. The 1898 *Report of Superintendent of Public Buildings and Grounds* noted that the chamber carpets had been taken up, cleaned, and put back down. The 1902 *Biennial Report* stated that a contract had been awarded for new carpeting in the chambers. *Report of Superintendent of Public Buildings and Grounds, Austin, November 1, 1898* (Austin: Von Boeckmann, Moore & Schutze, State Contractors, 1898), 4; *Biennial Report of the Superintendent of Public Buildings and Grounds, Austin, Texas, for Two Years Ending August 31, 1902* (Austin: Von Boeckmann, Schutze & Co., State Printers, 1902), 5. The original carpeting had lasted thirteen years. Subsequent replacements generally occurred every ten to fifteen years, the early patterning being adapted and eventually replaced by solid carpeting. The 1986 interim House chamber restoration reproduced the ca. 1905 carpet pattern, since the pattern of the original carpet could not be documented.

[67] *Specifications for Furnishing the New Capitol of Texas*, 1. Several other rooms in the Capitol received chairs identical to the members' chairs, including the secretary of state's private office. In 1941 the original members' chairs were replaced with fully upholstered models.

[68] *Specifications for Furnishing the New Capitol of Texas*, 1, 3; ibid., Exhibit titled "Robert Mitchell Furniture Company," 1, 3; A. H. Andrews and Company, *Commercial Furniture*, 74.

Figure 8. Myers's competition drawing which was titled, "Sketch Showing Finish of Supreme and Appellate Court Rooms." *Courtesy State Archives, Texas State Library.*

The photograph also documents elements in the room that were not included in the responsibilities of the Capitol Furnishing Board: wooden window shutters (referred to as "blinds" at that time), which were found on all above-ground Capitol windows; one of two large, star-shaped brass chandeliers and two of four corner brass chandeliers; two light standards at the president's platform; etched-glass ceiling panels; the gallery of paintings portraying men who had helped shape the destiny of the Empire State; and three composite photographs documenting the members of three legislative sessions (a practice that has continued to the present day).[69]

The E. E. Myers competition drawings for the construction of the Texas State Capitol include a sketch of the third floor Supreme Court-room, showing elaborate plaster decoration and frescoed motifs (fig. 8). It is not known if this ornamentation scheme was carried out; a 1904 photograph of the room, however, seems to show undecorated walls and ceiling (fig. 9).

---

[69] The fate of these items has been mixed: the brass chandeliers, composite photographs, and paintings have survived (for the most part); the light standards were removed by the 1920s; the wood blinds were taken down and replaced with window shades by 1929 and later with venetian blinds (a recent restoration returned wooden shutters to the chamber); the etched-glass ceiling panels were removed and the squares filled, eventually accommodating an air-conditioning system that was installed in 1957 (the majority of the panels have recently been reopened and plexiglass reproductions of the original glass panels installed).

Figure 9. The supreme courtroom, c. 1904. *Courtesy Austin History Center, Austin Public Library.*

The photograph documents much of the room's original furnishings. The small-scale, stylized floral carpeting is most likely the original body Brussels purchased for the room, since there are no references to a recarpeting of the area in earlier superintendent reports. The $125 draperies are similar in arrangement and trimming to the chamber examples.

The judges' stand, clerk's desk, "circle table," and several of the cuspidors and perforated armchairs specified for the room can be seen in the photograph. A view of the room circa 1925 provides a clearer image of the three judges' chairs, which were to be "rotary and spring, leather, with high backs," according to the *Specifications* (fig. 10).[70] The carved crest rail and general style of the chairs are extremely similar to one version of the popular perforated chair. The photograph also in-

---

[70] *Specifications for Furnishing the New Capitol of Texas*, 5. A "circle table" (actually a slightly curved table) was specified for each of the three courtrooms. At least two have survived and are currently in the John H. Reagan State Office Building, across the street from the north side of the Capitol.

Figure 10. The supreme courtroom, c. 1925. *Courtesy Austin History Center, Austin Public Library.*

cludes a better view of the clerk's desk, which matches the judges' stand in carving and detailing. One such desk has survived. Since it contains Andrews locks, it can be assumed that the judges' stand was also made by Andrews. Note that the carving on the judges' stand and clerk's desk is considerably more elaborate than that found on the clerk's desks and podiums in the chambers.

A 1950s photograph includes four of the eight wooden settees originally specified for the room (fig. 11).[71] The photograph also documents new chairs for the judges (whose number had increased to nine), fluorescent lighting, and, most striking, the relocation of the judges' stand to the other end of the room. The surrealistic wood surrounds framing the wall spaces on either side of the draperies actually frame sealed windows. The Supreme Court relocated to its newly constructed building in 1959. The judges' stand (and curtain rod) remain in the room, which is now used for committee meetings and hearings.

<hr />

[71] Ibid.

Figure 11. The supreme courtroom, c. 1955. *Courtesy State Archives, Texas State Library.*

A 1910 photograph of Judge William L. Davidson's third-floor room also includes a great deal of the original furniture (fig. 12). The five-foot-long table, rotary chair, revolving bookcase, mirrored wardrobe, cabinet washstand, two armchairs, and spittoon are all listed in the *Specifications.* Dozens of tables that match the judge's table were specified and purchased for the Capitol. Several of the tables have survived and contain Andrews locks. Two of the mirrored wardrobes have also survived and likewise have Andrews hardware. The judge's rotary chair and the two armchairs visible in the photograph are upholstered versions of the perforated armchairs (with five-hole pierced crest rail) that were used throughout the Capitol. Two wicker rockers are also located in the room. The *Specifications* listed one platform rocking chair, upholstered in leather, for each judge. Several of these leather rocking chairs have survived and are now located in the Supreme Court Building. Perhaps wicker rockers were provided as well, or they could be later additions to the room. Similarly, while only one revolving bookcase was specified for the judge's room, two (of different style) appear in the photograph.[72] Only a glimpse of another piece of furniture is visible in the photograph. A light-colored rail and cushion can be discerned in the lower right-hand corner. This is most likely one of the folding beds in its open position.

---

[72] Ibid.

Figure 12. Judge Davidson in his private room in the Capitol, c. 1910. *Courtesy State Archives, Texas State Library.*

The photograph of Governor Lanham circa 1903–1907 is the earliest known photograph of the governor's private office space, which was originally located on the first floor of the Capitol and included two rooms (fig. 1). This view of the southwest space documents both original furniture and later additions to the room.[73] The Austin *Daily Statesman* reported on November 27, 1901, that "Superintendent . . . Sam Harlan. . . . has placed an elegant new carpet in one of the governor's private offices. . . ."[74] Since the room with the desk undoubtedly received the most use (presumably the other room, for which no photograph exists, contained the more personal items, such as lounge, platform rockers, and wardrobe), it was probably the space recarpeted in 1901. This assumption is further substantiated by both the appearance and the pattern of the carpeting (more visible in a 1907–1911 photograph of Governor Thomas M. Campbell). The carpeting is in excel-

[73] Ibid., 11. The governor's private office was relocated to the second floor in 1935.
[74] Austin *Daily Statesman*, Nov. 27, 1901.

Figure 13. The Governor's business office in the early twentieth century. *Courtesy State Archives, Texas State Library.*

lent condition and has a repeating spiral pattern that seems closer to a 1900 than an 1890 design.

The 1898 *Biennial Report of the Superintendent of Public Buildings and Grounds* stated that the draperies in the governor's private offices had been relined.[75] The draperies in the Lanham photograph are probably the relined originals. The heavy fabric, tied back in "bishop sleeve" manner and trimmed with fringe and gigantic side tassels, clearly reflects Victorian drapery fashion.

The 1888 *Specifications* listed a curtain desk, table (2½ feet × 4 feet with billiard-cloth top), and twelve armchairs upholstered in leather for the office. The desk and table appear in the photograph, and four of the twelve chairs are visible.[76] The governor appears to be seated in a rotary version of the armchair, although no rotary chair had been specified, perhaps because of an oversight. Other features are additions to the room since the 1888 purchases: the table/file cabinet in the

---

[75] *Report of Superintendent of Public Buildings and Grounds . . . 1898*, p. 4.

[76] *Specifications for Furnishing the New Capitol of Texas*, 11. These chairs are also seen in other Capitol photographs, including ones of the governor's business office, a judge's room, and a judiciary clerk's office. Two of the armchairs were recently discovered and were purchased for the State Preservation Board by the nonprofit fundraising organization The Capitol Committee, Inc. The table is located in the Administration Building at Texas Tech University in Lubbock.

Figure 14. The Comptroller's office in the early twentieth century. *Courtesy Austin History Center, Austin Public Library.*

corner; the dictionary stand; and the second swivel chair (which may have been pulled into the room for the meeting or the photograph). Likewise, the window shades, lighting, and ceiling fan are later additions. Despite the massive carved desk, the room nevertheless seems rather simple, considering that it is part of the governor's private office space.

The governor's business office was a large room comfortably fitted with office furniture. An early twentieth-century photograph of the room conforms for the most part to the plan originally specified (fig. 13). The photograph reveals one of the three curtain desks and four of the twelve leather armchairs, as well as the water cooler, wardrobe, table, revolving bookcase, and metal unit with three hundred pigeonholes for boxes, all listed in the *Specifications*. The patterned linoleum simulating an encaustic tile design dates to late 1900. On January 1, 1901, the Austin *Daily Statesman* reported that the superintendent had just completed the installation of new linoleum in the business office.[77]

A more typical office scene is captured in an early photograph of one of the many offices of the comptroller, which were located on the first

[77] Ibid.; Austin *Daily Statesman*, Jan. 1, 1901.

floor of the northeast wing (fig. 14). Functional wood furniture and metal shelving units are arranged where most needed, with little apparent consideration for aesthetics. Desks and tables are cluttered with the work of the day. Natural sunlight is supplemented by one of the brass chandeliers installed throughout the building toward the end of the nineteenth century (in his 1896 *Biennial Report,* the superintendent reported that ten new chandeliers had been installed in the Capitol; the 1898 *Biennial Report* listed the installation of fifty chandeliers).[78]

A discussion of Capitol furnishings and interiors would not be complete without the inclusion of the governor's public reception room (figs. 15, 16). Many features indicate the special importance attached to the room, centered at the front of the building on the second floor. Historically, the room located in such a position was considered the most important one in the building. Also, while the woodwork throughout the Capitol was primarily oak or pine, that in the governor's area was either walnut or mahogany, with cherry only in the Reception Room.

The superior quality and higher cost of the room's draperies and carpeting have been noted. The furniture specified was also finer than items requested for other Capitol rooms. Clearly patterned after a parlor, the room was to receive two sofas, eight rockers ("all different"), ten chairs, a "centre table with Tennessee marble top," four stands "on which to place flowers, etc.," a pier glass (a large, free-standing, framed mirror), and a "silver ewer for water, with cups and a suitable stand."[79]

Some redecorating took place in 1898. On April 12, 1898, the Austin *Daily Tribune* reported: "All the furniture has been reupholstered and the magnificent curtains that cost $700 per pair, have been relined with silk. . . ." A few months later, the Austin *Daily Statesman* noted the changes as well: "The chairs are fresh from the upholsterer, and the beautiful draperies in the windows have been relined in gold with pretty fancy work."[80] A circa 1900 photograph (fig. 15) shows the new

---

[78] *Report of Superintendent of Public Buildings and Grounds . . . 1898,* p. 4; *Report of Superintendent of Public Buildings and Grounds, Austin, November 1, 1896* (Austin: Ben C. Jones & Co., State Printers, 1896), 4. Depending on the size of the room, chandeliers with four, six, or eight arms with shades were purchased. The State Preservation Board is in the process of reproducing these chandeliers for areas undergoing restoration.

[79] *Specifications for Furnishing the New Capitol of Texas,* 12.

[80] Austin *Daily Tribune,* Apr. 12, 1898 (1st quotation); Austin *Daily Statesman,* June 10, 1898 (2nd quotation). An earlier report in the *Statesman* had not been so complimentary: "the furnishing recalls the gorgeous drapery of 'Bossy' on her first full-dress in Hoyt's play of the 'Texas Steer'; and with all due respect for the sovereign lawmakers of Texas, I would suggest that they 'shoot' the decorations in the governor's room, and if they cannot do better, to hire some school boy who has taken his first lesson in drawing and color mixing to replace them. . . . the present trappings are a hideous concoction of loud and glaring colors with neither beauty of design nor harmony of assembly." Ibid., May 5, 1892.

fabrics selected for the upholstered furniture. The most noticeable change is the replacement of a floral pattern with a striped design on the four side chairs. The photograph also documents the silver water ewer and stand listed in the *Specifications* and includes three crystal vases and two spittoons. The fringe and massive tie-back tassels of the original draperies are also clearly detailed in the photograph.

Although termed a "public" reception area, the room apparently saw only infrequent use, being set aside for special occasions just as a best parlor in a home would have been reserved for guests. Newspaper accounts record notable events that have occurred in the room over the years. When former Governor Oran M. Roberts died in May, 1898, his body lay in state in the reception room, "which was opened to callers during the day." In 1899 William Jennings Bryan received the public in the room, "giving hundreds of ladies and gentlemen the opportunity to call upon the distinguished silver orator." In 1936, after a Centennial-inspired restoration, the first event held in the room "was the signing of Miss Janice Jarratt, 'sweetheart' of the Centennial, to a Hollywood film contract."[81]

The lack of constant use made it possible for the room to remain relatively intact for several years. The original carpeting was not replaced until 1910, at which time the furniture was reupholstered. The 1910 carpeting was not replaced for twenty-six years, by which time it was "literally in holes. It almost fell to pieces as it was removed."[82]

Despite later remodelings (fig. 16), several pieces of original furniture have remained in the room. The matching center table, pier mirror, and two of the four pedestals have survived.[83] The S-curved bench, known as a tête-à-tête, was not listed in the original *Specifications* but appears in the earliest photograph of the room, dated 1894. At some point (1950s or 1960s) it was moved to the Governor's Mansion and later placed in storage. A 1986 restoration returned the tête-à-tête to the reception room.[84]

---

[81] Austin *Daily Statesman*, May 21 1898, Mar. 9, 1899, Sept. 23, 1936.

[82] *Biennial Report of the Superintendent of Public Buildings and Grounds, Austin, Texas, for Two Years Ending August 31, 1910* (Austin: Austin Printing Company, 1910), 3; Austin *Daily Statesman*, Sept. 23, 1936.

[83] For years stories have been told about the table and mirror that do not appear to have any basis in fact. The wood in the table is claimed to be a gift from the descendants of Davy Crockett. The mirror is said to be a gift from the Republic of France, and one of the "most perfect" mirrors in the world. The table's connection to Crockett has probably been based on the notation in the *Specifications* that the top of the table was to contain "Tennessee marble." The *Specifications* also stated that mirrors must be of "French plate," a term indicating a type of mirror, not its place of origin.

[84] The restoration project, made possible thanks to a $100,000 grant from the Heritage Society of Austin, also reproduced the original carpeting and draperies, returned the 1898 chan-

What general conclusions can be made about the selections of the Capitol Furnishing Board? What influenced its decisions? Contemporary reports and commentaries do not address these broader issues, but a few assumptions can be made from the available evidence.

It is known that the board members and their expert advisor, architect Nicholas Clayton, were aware of the furnishing plans for other state capitols. The 1886 *Biennial Report of the Capitol Building Commission* noted that they had amassed a great deal of information about the furnishings of several capitol buildings.[85] Certainly this information was not completely overlooked during the decision-making process.

The budgetary restrictions could have seriously affected the quality of the furnishings, yet the board handled this problem by only furnishing what it considered priority areas. The report states that the board felt the areas furnished were appropriately done.[86] Indeed, the newspapers had always been the harshest critics during this project, yet they had nothing but the highest praise for the selections of the board.

It is also important to reiterate that A. H. Andrews and Company was the leading American manufacturer of office furniture in the country. It supplied furnishings for many important public buildings of the period. Certainly its products would have been among the most popular on the market. Equally, quality materials and workmanship were foremost in the minds of the board members. The report detailed the reason that delivery of the furniture was delayed: it all had to be custom-made because of the requirement that it meet U.S. government specifications, which were generally not followed in the manufacture of furniture.[87]

A survey of the dozens of interior Capitol photographs that have been discovered to date reveals that the rooms were furnished with well-designed, up-to-date, quality oak and walnut office furniture. The Capitol occupants had nothing to be ashamed of when they moved into their new offices. The amount of furniture might seem to have been a bit sparse, but it has to be remembered that the building was at first much larger than it needed to be for the functions of the state; the number of employees and not the amount of available square footage dictated how much furniture was purchased for each room.

---

delier to the room (it had been removed in the 1960s), and placed additional Victorian furniture in the room to complement the surviving original pieces.

[85] *Third Biennial Report of the Capitol Building Commission*, 5.

[86] *Report of the Capitol Furnishing Board*, 9.

[87] Ibid., 7.

Figure 15. The Governor's public reception room, c. 1894 (top) and in 1900 (bottom). *Top courtesy of State Archives, Texas State Library. Bottom courtesy Barker Texas History Center, University of Texas at Austin.*

Figure 16. The Governor's public reception room in 1939 (top) and in 1988 (bottom). *Courtesy State Archives, Texas State Library.*

It must be admitted, however, that the more important rooms—namely, those assigned to the governor—were not as well furnished as one would have expected. Despite the fact that two to three times as much money was spent on the carpeting, draperies, and furnishings in these areas, they were still not as finely appointed as comparable spaces in other Capitols, including California, Colorado, and Michigan. True, the governor's desk was nearly the same as that owned by wealthy businessman Marshall Field; yet the photographs of the governor's office reveal a rather simply furnished space. Likewise, the governor's public reception room, while furnished more grandly than any space in the building, was nevertheless much less splendidly furnished than fine Austin parlors of the 1880s.[88] Both the Colorado and Michigan governors' reception rooms were more elaborately furnished than the Texas equivalent.

Yet no suggestion can be found in any newspaper accounts or other commentaries that Texas had in any way inappropriately furnished its Capitol. The emphasis on function, practicality, and sound quality seems to have been acceptable to and expected by the Texan citizenry. These values are also evident in the building's interior architecture: the undecorated woodwork, walls, and ceilings, the geometric encaustic tile flooring, and the simple brass chandeliers and sconces added later reflect an appreciation and preference for a more basic beauty determined by quality and function rather than unnecessary decoration and elaborate materials.

As early as the first decades of the twentieth century, the combination of increasing demands for office space, insufficient maintenance funds, and modern needs and tastes gradually began to change the original interior appearance of the Capitol. In 1887 a reporter who toured the nearly completed building had commented on the vast amount of available room: "Each state officer will have five times more space in this building than he ever had before. And there are a great many splendid rooms on this floor . . . for departments that do not yet exist. . . ."[89] The rooms quickly filled up, however, and by 1914 the *Biennial Report of the Superintendent of Public Buildings and Grounds* addressed the seriousness of the space shortage:

I wish to impress home the fact that if the legislature continues to create new boards and new offices, that some provision must be made for housing the new

---

[88] A finer parlor of the nineteenth century was located in the Henry Hirschfeld house at 303 West 9th Street in Austin. For photographic reference, see House File #303 West 9th in the photographic files at the Austin History Center, Austin Public Library.

[89] Austin *Daily Statesman*, Dec. 29, 1887.

officials. . . . At this time there are 20 committee rooms being occupied by 11 state departments . . . on account of a lack of other quarters. . . . It has become necessary to close the west end of the corridor on the ground floor in order to make working room for additional forces that have been quartered by law in the Capitol building.[90]

Maintenance funds were continually in meager supply. In 1898 the Austin *Daily Tribune* commented:

The legislature made a $2,500 appropriation for repairs while congress made a $55,000 appropriation for repairs in the National Capitol. Superintendent [John R.] Mobley says the legislature must make a larger appropriation to keep the building in proper repair.[91]

The last century has taken its toll on the Capitol interiors, yet the basic grandeur of the building is intact. The ongoing restoration project will return many rooms to a late Victorian ambience more in keeping with the original furnishings specifications and purchases. As the Austin *Daily Statesman* pointed out over one hundred years ago:

This capitol will not only be the pride of the state of Texas but of this country, and it is only mete [*sic*] and proper that it should be furnished in a manner somewhat in conformity with the grandeur and magnificence of its appearance.[92]

---

[90] *Biennial Report of the Superintendent of Public Buildings and Grounds for the Two Years Ending August 31, 1914* (Austin: Von Boeckmann–Jones Co., Printers, 1914), 4.

[91] Austin *Daily Tribune*, Apr. 12, 1898.

[92] Austin *Daily Statesman*, Mar. 4, 1887.

Index